Parental Alienation Survival Coach

Healing, humor, heart, poetry, prayers, verses, self-care and a 6-step program to be better, not bitter!

MONICA GIGLIO

Copyright © 2017 Published by

Speak Worldwide 501c3

All rights reserved.

ISBN:
ISBN-9781717895769

DEDICATION

Dedicated to my children and to my late parents from whom I learned how to put a square peg in a round hole and never give up on anything. Also to every alienated parent and child, especially those who bravely share their stories with others. May they find solace, comfort, laughs, hope and healing in the pages of this book.

INTRODUCTION

Family separation happens to millions of good, law abiding, citizens, often facilitated by "Family Court" systems. Can you imagine what it's like to NOT have the phone number, address, or email of your own children, and be blocked from all forms of social media? You can, if you are an alienated, erased, or amputated parent.

Do you know what it's like to enter your own child's name into an internet search to satisfy your natural urge to know if they are dead or alive? Do you know what it's like to not be able to comfort your child in their struggles, or even know if they are having struggles? Do you know what it's like to not be able to say Happy Birthday or send a card or gift to them? You do if your child has been psychologically abused to hate, reject, mistrust, and fear you, and believe you are a threat and you deserve to be punished.

Do you know what it's like for a young child to be ripped out of your life while only a toddler? Do you know what it's like when your children devote large portions of their time to making sure you don't find them to express your love or desire to be part of their lives? You do, if you have seen the normal, healthy, mutually loving bonds you once had, shattered and broken.

Parental Alienation often includes bullying, domestic violence, and psychological abuse to shatter normal parent/child bonds. The catastrophic results in children tormented this way can lead to self hatred, teen pregnancy, depression, gang involvement, susceptibility to predators, eating disorders, and youth suicide (sadly some as young as 11 years old). Chronic stress, traumatic prolonged grief, and helplessness overcome parents whose children have been enlisted in coalitions against them. After devoting their lives to trying to reverse this tragedy, parents who feel their lives have lost their meaning, often become withdrawn, passive and suicidal.

To offer hope, the YouTube channel and Facebook Group "Parental Alienation Survival Coach" are making positive differences in the lives of broken-hearted people around the globe, and Speak Worldwide 501c3, offers a mission of education, compassion, and spiritual renewal thru support groups, fact sheets, and books.

The eerily similar stories from thousands of crushed people all over the world have catalyzed the passion to write this book. Parental Alienation Survival Coach captures the feelings of shock, confusion and helplessness that parents experience as they are pushed out of their children's lives, and their desperate struggle for education to understand what's happening. Follow along on every alienated parent's journey from crushing heartbreak, to wellness, despite significant open wounds. Chapters alternate from sad, to funny, to inspirational, to hopeful and include healing, humor, heart, prayers, verses, self-care and my exclusive 6-step program! Names have been changed to protect privacy and any similarities are coincidental.

CONTENTS

	Introduction	iv
	Acknowledgments	vii
1	Awakening	1
2	Love Her As Hard As You Can	11
3	A Good Year	15
4	Push Past the Broken Pieces	23
5	Love Letters Wall	31
6	Bubblegum In the Tank	67
7	Gram-mum Hates You	69
8	The Big Blue Can	75
9	Freezer Bra	79
10	Broken Hearts and Poems of Solace	83
11	Avalanches of Life	93
12	Daddy Doesn't Love Me	97
13	House Song	101
14	Reverse Engineering	105
15	It Hurts	109
16	Thinking Dreams	117

17	Christmas Angel	119
18	Online Support Groups	123
19	Living Life Forward	151
20	Five Phases of Grief	155
21	Self-Care	161
22	Six-Step Plan	167
23	Testimonials	171

ACKNOWLEDGMENTS

Many thanks to my editor Lisa who helped me move forward on this project, and to all those who offered critique prior to launch. I am very grateful to the body of family therapy experts who have dedicated much of their work and research to this sensitive and sad topic who have informed my understanding, so that I may compassionately offer help, hope and healing. Some contributors are no longer with us, but have left their imprint on this field of study. I have purchased many of their books, participated in their surveys and feverishly studied their public domain works, some of which are quoted in this book:

        Dr. Amy JL Baker
        Dr. William Bernet
        Dr. Michael Bone
        Murray Bowen
        Linda Gottlieb
        Dr. Lorenzo Lorandos
        Dr. Jane Major
        Dr. Steven Miller
        Salvador Minuchin
        Ryan Thomas
        Dr. Richard Warshak
        Karen Woodall

Finally, thanks to everyone, all over the world, who has been encouraging me for many years, to finally "write a book!"

1 AWAKENING

Parents all over the world are awakening to a nightmare their children have endured or are enduring, a process of lies and twisted truths that may include bullying and cult-like strategies to break down and ultimately destroy the normal, healthy parent/child bond they've shared. If you are an awakening parent who is suffering damage to, or the loss of life's greatest relationships, you are experiencing a myriad of sometimes crippling emotions for which you are unprepared. You may feel 'caught in the headlights' and frozen or overwhelmed with powerlessness after trying without success, everything you could think of to restore normal, loving relationships with your children. One of your greatest needs is to know you are not alone, and reading this book should bring you the comfort that millions of other parents understand the shock and bewilderment of being hit with a gut-wrenching pain you didn't see coming. Sadly your initial pain may be followed by false judgment and accusations when you confide your biggest heartbreak to friends and family who lack the capacity to understand and think you contributed to making your children act as if they hate you. Throughout this book, the rejected parent is assumed to be a normal, loving, healthy available parent.

Family Separation is a phrase commonly used for criminals who are being processed while their children receive care. Sympathy flows from many normal caring people who realize how painful this separation must feel. However, Parental Alienation is a phrase that has been met with controversy over the years to describe what has always been known in psychological literature as a form of Child Psychological Abuse. The following description will help you understand what is mean by Parental Alienation throughout this book:

> *"Parental Alienation is the process, and the result, of the psychological manipulation of a child into showing unwarranted fear, disrespect or hostility towards a parent or other family members… It is a distinctive and widespread form of psychological abuse and family violence, towards both the child and the rejected family members, that occurs almost exclusively in association with family separation or divorce …"* ~Wikipedia quote from top experts, Dr. Amy JL Baker, Dr. William Bernet, Dr. Lorenzo Lorandos, and Dr. Richard Warshak.

If you have not personally encountered this kind of loss and devastation, this book is also for you. Chances are there is at least one parent and child/

children in your life circle, workplace, neighborhood, or church who need your help as they are suffering in secret silence, the chronic grief and complex trauma that result from the tragedy referred to as Parental Alienation. They need your help and understanding.

It occurs when one parent wishes for their child's other parent to be erased out of their children's lives and perceived as a common enemy and threat. To make that wish come true, they often choose a path of lies and destruction with severe consequences. When adults pull children into their cross-generational coalition against their other parent it is known in psychology as a "perverse triangle"; a toxic involvement of innocent children in adult matters, covertly persuading them to perceive the other parent in violation of court-orders and as unworthy of love. Prominent family therapy and psychiatry pioneers such as Murray Bowen and Salvador Minuchin have linked it to maladjustment in children.

How does a child go from feelings of safety and resting comfortably in the loving arms of a parent, to despising them in the strongest way? To various degrees, they are shamed, mocked and punished for feelings of love, affection, and desire toward a parent and often that entire side of family. They are rewarded for disparaging, disrespecting and dismissing their normal loving parent, and taught that parent is not worthy of love, affection, attention, or access.

> *"The kids hear a steady drumbeat about a parent's flaws and lies that portray one parent as unloving and unworthy of love,"*
> ~Dr. Richard Warshak, psychiatry professor and author of **Divorce Poison**.

Children all over the world are awakening too. Several now-adult children are emerging to share their stories and help parents and other kids. Some, like Ryan Thomas offer multiple free resources that give parents a peak into the minds of alienated children traingulated into a cross-generational coalition by what he calls "the regime" that included his mother and other family members to make him view his dad as their common enemy and threat. Most children don't realize they've been "brainwashed" to align with one parent, and are being used in a scheme to hurt or even destroy the other. Some are expected to call their step-parent "mom" or "dad" and refer to their real parent "the thing" or some other derogatory phrase.

One now-adult child put it like this: "I went through a stage as a child when I was being alienated from my mother. I didn't know what Parental Alienation was until years later when it happened to me in my divorce. I used to join in on the making fun of my mother when my dad, step-mom or grandmother would call her a loser, deadbeat, lazy, fake, etc. I remember feeling guilty about it but I also felt like if I agreed with them and acted out against my mother, my dad and step-mom would be easier on me, treat me better, and love me more. If I acted like I loved or missed my mother they'd yell and call me a loser like her, then and make fun of me. There was no way out, and I didn't understand it, 'till now as its happening to me."

Another child put it this way. "My dad, whom I lived with, made me write letters to my mom saying I don't ever want to see her again. I was told to write that I hated her and didn't need her involved in my life in any way. He then monitored every phone call and text if she tried to reach out to me. I was under orders to basically treat her like I hated her, and ignore her or respond hurtfully to her. He told me so many lies about her and while they didn't make sense, I also didn't want to believe that he was lying. I was very confused. But one thing I did know was that deep down, I did love my mother. I wasn't allowed to be in touch with that authentic emotion or other ones. I was made to feel ashamed of my feelings. I missed out on many years with not only my mom, but also all my cousins, aunts, uncles, and even my grandparents died while I was alienated from my mom. There is no way I can get that time back."

Hearing the stories from formerly alienated kids helps explain how and why children begin to adopt whatever irrational lies and false narratives they are told by the parent who has gained psychological control over them and monitors like a prison guard their phone calls and texts from their other parent. Unfortunately, these dynamics leave very little opportunity to help the child out of the quagmire while they are still under the sphere of influence of the embittered parent. You cannot approach a child with rational information about Parental Alienation and expect them to understand they are being psychologically manipulated as if in a cult. They would be very intimidated about challenging their parent who gained psychological control over them from a young age. Some children will defensively and reflexively reply with something like "I decided to cut my parent out of my life all by myself! No one told me to feel this way!" However, their reasons are based on lies from the other parent, frivolous, unjustified, and not based in any valid experiences with the healthy parent, who did nothing to contribute to severing the eternal parent/child bond. As they mature into adults, some children eventually come to their own awakening and realize their parent wasn't the psycho, addict, stealer of child support money, loser or phony they'd been led to believe. When the children begin to have their awakening, it is the start of a very painful and difficult journey toward the truth. So difficult, that some children find it easier to remain in the lies they'd been told their whole lives.

Adding to a parent's pain when their child is being taught to hate, reject, and fear them, is the commonly held notion that two high conflict parents are to blame, but this is usually not true. In most cases of severe alienation it is one cooperative, compromising, easy to get along with, empathetic, caring and really nice parent with great people skills, and one parent who rejects the truth that children want, deserve, need and have the RIGHT to love and be loved by both parents and both sides of the family. That parent gains psychological control of the child's mind and triangulates them into adult-conflict with lies and twisted truths, conditioning them to hate, reject, and fear the other parent and often the entire side of the family. Although it often manifests in custody battles, it is not about contact with, or custody of the children.

> *"Parental alienation is not about contact, it is not a problem about high conflict, it is an issue in which our first act has to be to ensure the child's safety and our second act has to be to protect and rebuild the child's relationship with their healthy parent."* ~ Karen Woodall, internationally recognized psychotherapist on the phenomenon of the alienated child.

Dr. Amy J L Baker is also an internationally known expert on Parental Alienation, and puts 17 primary alienation strategies employed by embittered parents all over the world into **5 general categories**:
1. Poisonous messages to the child about the targeted parent in which he or she is portrayed as unloving, unsafe, and unavailable;
2. Limiting contact and communication between the child and the targeted parent;
3. Erasing and replacing the targeted parent in the heart and mind of the child;
4. Encouraging the child to betray the targeted parent's trust;
5. Undermining the authority of the targeted parent.

It's important to note a simple truth that Dr. Jayne Major made very clear when she said, "We know that normal people don't do this to their children." Most experts agree feelings of human inadequacy and fears of abandonment drive the alienation strategies. Seen in millions of cases around the world, these bullying and cult-like strategies result in **8 behavioral manifestations**:
1. Campaign of denigration against the targeted parent
2. Weak, frivolous, or absurd reasons for the rejection of the targeted parent;
3. Lack of ambivalence towards both parents in which one is viewed as all good and the targeted parent as all bad;
4. Lack of remorse for the poor treatment of the targeted parent;
5. Reflexive support for the favored parent;
6. Use of borrowed scenarios; (scenarios they never experienced)

7. The "independent thinker" phenomenon; and
8. Spread of animosity towards the friends and family of the targeted parent.

When parents awaken to these behaviors in their once sweet, loving, caring children, the reality of Parental Alienation is upon them. Many parents scurry to educate themselves and hope for early intervention or prevention of this nightmare. Over time, they discover scholarly articles and videos leading to moments of "Ah-ha! I am not alone! There is a actually a name for it." In the following chapters, you will ride along with them on the roller-coaster of emotions as they try to understand what is happening and why they feel so powerless to change what has already been set it motion, like a snowball rolling faster and larger downhill. If you are an awakening parent you will identify with the emotions and find solace, hope and solutions to improve your life. <u>Most importantly to your well-being, you will know you are not alone!</u>

Approximately 22 million parents struggle with the confusion and all the emotions in the nightmare referred to as Parental Alienation. Propelled by my Christian faith and the hope it provides, I try hard to continue living my life in a positive, forward-moving, direction. Because I believe that suffering and heartache can lead us to growth and learning, I have always been one to search for purpose in pain, and a way to redeem it. Usually that purpose involves helping others, as 2nd Corinthians 1:4 says of God,

"He comforts us in all our troubles so that we can comfort others. When they are troubled, we will be able to give them the same comfort God has given us."

As an educator and former technical writer, I've always been able to deliver difficult information in ways lay people can easily understand. For many years I've educated and shared understanding across multiple social media platforms, via posts and self-help, compassionate, and educational videos. To help parents find their path to healing, I have been encouraged to write a book like this for a long time.

I chose to write in non-linear format and although many chapters are written in my voice, this book is not my story. It is the eerily similar stories from millions of parents from all over the world. Normal people with otherwise-normal lives find themselves in the freakishly abnormal situation of being rejected without any justification by their children who have been caught in a web of lies. I've included art, poetry, prayers, and previously published humor and feel-good stories to lighten this sad topic and help give a more complete picture of individuals whose lives are full, and whose only 'crime' is wanting a normal relationship with their children. I've also included helpful, actionable chapters on self-care, grief processing, and my unique 6-step program for alienated parents to become better, not bitter. Names have been changed to protect and respect individual privacy, and any similarities are coincidental.

The Heart of a Child
Unknown Author

The heart of a child is a scroll,
A page that is lovely and white;
And to it as fleeting years roll,
Come hands with a story to write.

Be ever so careful, O hand,
Write thou with a sanctified pen;
Thy story shall live in the land
For years, in the doings of men.

It shall echo in circles of light,
Or lead to the death of a soul.
Give here but a message right,
On the heart of your child: a scroll.

2 LOVE HER AS HARD AS YOU CAN
Originally published in The Showcase Magazine

"Love Her As Hard As You Can"... That was the admonition given me as I parted company with an elderly lady in the checkout line, whom I remember as Checkout Granny. She was a proper English woman with silver waves and crystal blues. Frail and aged, she maintained proper carriage, her head high and her shoulders back. My infant daughter, with shining black hair, flawless porcelain skin, rosy cheeks, and round dark eyes framed by long curling eyelashes, smiled and cooed, and this delightful stranger could not contain herself. "Oh my God!" she exclaimed as her jaw dropped. In excited admiration she added, "She looks just like a china doll!" I smiled proudly, blushed, and thanked her for her compliment. I was lucky that way. Looking at my children brought joy to strangers, and when they expressed it to me, my heart and soul swelled with maternal fulfillment, and my world was good. On days when I had three little ones in - and alongside - the shopping cart, I would be approached by other strangers who could not resist the urge to tell me how sweet and beautiful they were, and even more flattering, how well behaved and happy they seemed. I felt blessed and privileged my children were not only a precious gift to me, but to others also, if only for a passing moment. Checkout Granny was not the first to tell me she did a double-take to make sure baby Amy was real and not a china doll.

When I gave birth to her, I knew she would change me. "Her name is Amy Paulette and she will change my life forever...," I wrote in my journal. She was my second child, but my first daughter. Indeed her perfection made me see my own imperfection in a bright light, and made me want to banish all my flaws. She did change me; her presence inspired me to do better and strive to be the best I could. She was a happy, content, bright-eyed, and angelic baby who barely ever cried. Loving her was the easiest thing in the world.

When Checkout Granny, full of passion and great emotion, said to me, "Oh, love her as hard as you can, dear. Always love this precious bundle just as hard as you possibly can", I took those words home with me. I pondered them over and over. I had never before, nor since, heard anyone ever put it quite that way. I wondered if she was implying something left unsaid, like "because you never know how long you will have her". I wondered if maybe she'd lost a child in its infancy, and knew all too well how precious and fleeting life is. Or maybe she knew only restrained love by her own mother, who perhaps had held back, not fully embracing the high calling of motherhood. Maybe she herself had not given her all to her own children, and regretted the broken relationships her negligence produced. Or maybe she never had the precious miracle of children in her life at all. I will never really know what inspired the words Checkout Granny left me with that day, but I do know I never wanted to have any regrets. Because loving Amy was as natural as drinking a glass of water, I wondered sometimes if I was doing it hard enough. As a gentle reminder to be the best mother I could be, I would ask myself if I was giving her everything I've got, everything she deserved. Loving Amy was easy, but I wanted to do it as hard as I could.

Now that my children are teenagers, I understand like many of you have discovered, love is hard sometimes. Making the right decisions for them, and helping them learn to make right choices for themselves, are not as easy as drinking a glass of water anymore. It's a time of second-guessing yourself as a parent, and wondering if you've been too strict, or too permissive. You want their dreams to come true, you want them to be happy and successful in the long run. And, you want them to enjoy the journey and have fun along the way as they grow into adults. Loving them comes in the form of giving them freedoms, along with responsibilities, respecting their boundaries and learning to let go a little at a time. Loving them sometimes means watching them make their own mistakes and getting hurt, even when you feel their pain more than they do. Loving them demands patience, self-reflection, and flexibility. Loving them requires deliberate efforts on sometimes precarious footing as you help navigate them through life. And sometimes it means letting them think you are dumb and letting them think they hate you for the unpopular decisions you make. It can be very frustrating and sometimes very hard to know if you are doing "love" right.

Is this what Checkout Granny really meant? After all these years, her words still echo as a reminder to me and perhaps to all of us with children, now more than ever; "Love her as hard as you can…".

3 A GOOD YEAR

Katy Begins Her Awakening With Her Year End Letter...
Happy Holidays Everyone!
    All in all 2016 has been a good year. In February, I celebrated my birthday surrounded by lots of friends and family in a flapper-and-gangtser-themed party at a restaurant I'd helped and launch, followed by an overnight stay at the Jersey Shore with close friends. In the Spring, I grew a beautiful flower garden that provided vibrant color for many months, and a vegetable garden, which was weak by comparison, but produced a few now-famous cucumbers! In the summer I traveled cross-country from Washington to Florida in an RV with two of my best friends making many memories, and further forging the bonds of friendship.
    This year I also began a series of stained glass pieces dealing with human suffering and overcoming pain. I sold several pieces and produced many more. I had a solo art show at a gallery in Tribeca. I hosted Thanksgiving, Christmas Eve, and even threw an impromptu quiet New Year's Eve party, in addition to regular Wednesday dinners with friends in my home. Despite my cancer recovery, I have remained

somewhat productive, and although I do have very bad days mixed in, I try not to focus on them and keep my mind as active as possible.

Love still eludes me in the biggest way. Despite another year of giving online dating a good "college try" and generally putting myself out there, I still have not developed a significant love relationship after all these years as a single mom. But without question, the biggest way love eludes me and what hurts most, was losing the love of my 19 - and 20 - year old daughters, their alienation from me, and their final separation when they were 16. I hadn't believed the bonds of love between daughters and their mothers could break; that a daughter's love for a normal, caring mother could be destroyed by the influence of their father, stepfamily, and Gramma. But it happened; like the branches in full Autumn glory bent low with the accumulation of an early, heavy October snow this year, some snapped back upright shaking the snow off their colorful leaves like confetti, while others cracked from the weight of it all and broke, fully severed from the trunk of the trees.

Looking back, I see it was like a cancer that comes gradually and silently while you ignore, minimize, and diminish the bumps and lumps, until one day you are faced with severe damage to your being and a life-threatening illness. That's what's happened this year. I realized I have a "cancer". Mario, whose depression and seething hatred of me dominated our marriage, had threatened before our divorce, "I'm gonna make sure these kids know exactly what I think of you, and by the time they are teenagers they will hate you too." I pitied him for being a hater, but didn't believe he had the power to make that and other threats come true. Perhaps I was in denial. But I chose to focus on the power of pure love instead, to overcome all evil, and I kept moving forward.

I'd embraced motherhood from the start with every ounce of my being. I formed playgroups, and made parenting my priority. I took my children to beaches, parks, apple and pumpkin picking. Being divorced when they were little didn't change my passion for parenting. I saved my pennies for vacations and road trips. I hosted craft parties, birthday parties and sleepovers. I bought them computers, electronics, phones, and party dresses for the many formal celebrations to which they were invited. I made sure they had good relationships with doctors, teachers, administrators, guidance staff and other adults. I was involved in their schools as are all caring patents, and I was a milk-n-cookies mom with home cooked meals every night. I continued to provide a loving home where their friends were always welcome. I coached sports and Annie became a star basketball player in high school. I somehow found the money to send Jill to Spain as part of an exchange program in her sophomore year. I took them to church and installed strong faith, work, and education ethics that catalyzed their development into honor students and hard-working individuals with part-time jobs throughout high school and into college. I even helped them shop for Mario, their stepmom and step-siblings at holiday time and brought them to visit Mario's mother and grandmother to keep family values a priority.

Over the years my friends had observed whenever Jill and Annie returned from weekends, holidays, or vacations with Mario, they were angry, conflicted and distant. I brushed it off as normal difficulty in transitioning from one household to another. In hindsight, I now understand they were struggling with the perception of me as an all-bad and worthless person under Marios's influence, colliding with the reality that I displayed normal, healthy, loving, parental ways. "Cognitive dissonance" is what they experienced every time they were with me. It's the internal conflict that arises when what you've been told, doesn't match up with what you experience, and almost impossible for children to process.

While married, Mario mocked three year old Tom for crying on my shoulder. "Ohhh the baby has to run to his Mommy? Look at the little sissy, the Mama's boy." This refrain resurfaced again when Jill called me from a visit to his house, excited to tell me she lost her first tooth. "Ohhh look at the baby who has to call her Mommy…" I now know it's a common form of parental psychological abuse to shame children for loving, showing and receiving affection from a normal, healthy, loving parent. There are many other ways Mario made it painful, even shameful, for our children to love and care about me, or want to buy me gifts for holidays, birthdays, or Mother's Day.

When Annie and Tom, seven and eight years old at the time, felt unsafe riding around in the trunk portion of Mario's SUV so he could fit all the children and stepchildren in one car instead of taking two cars to church and other places, they told me about it. "He makes us duck down whenever there's a police car around, so he doesn't get sent to jail!" He scolded and shamed them for telling me they were afraid for their safety and admonished, "It's none of HER business what you do when you are visiting me. She'll have me arrested and thrown in jail!" He also forbade them from saying anything to me about their time with him, and from bringing any of their toys, clothes, possessions or gifts back and forth to our home. I'd once packaged up a few toys and things for them to keep at his house, and later learned he tossed it all into his basement, calling it "a bag of junk from your mother." I've since learned that's another common devaluation tactic. In a slow, insidious way, Tom and Annie were made to feel I was insignificant; and worse, they began to adopt his hatred as their own, and perceive me as an enemy without any justification. When they became adolescents and began to naturally individuate, they added their own anger to the scaffolding prepared for them and were enjoined into a pact with their father. "You only have to put up with your mother until you are 16. Then you can leave her for good and never have to speak to her, hear from her, or look at her again." It took a while for me to know anything about this campaign against me, and even when I found out, I didn't believe it would come true. Children need their moms, I thought.

In time, Annie and Tom began to parrot the abusive accusations I'd heard from Mario while we'd been married. Without any evidential or experiential history, they called me a "psycho" (one of his favorites), sociopathic, abusive and an addict, and said their awards dinners, proms, and high school graduation ceremonies were none of my business. And so, although they lived mostly with me and went to school in our town, they demanded I stop attending their sporting events and teacher's meetings. They said I never should have had kids, and that 16 years with me was long enough, just like their father. That's how Tom put it in a note I found on the floor of his empty bedroom, the day she left to move in with Mario full-time at age 16. "F-U. 16 years was long enough, just like it was for my father and my sister!", he wrote. He'd previously schemed that, "when both of us are gone, then everyone will know it's YOU that has a problem!" Indicating it was part of their conjured plan, she continued "With BOTH kids leaving you, no one will believe you are normal! Have fun with that. Have fun not knowing if we get married, or have kids, or are even alive." They seemed to have a need to prove their love for Mario by showing they feel the same way toward me that he does. They have also been avoiding all my family, many old friends who do not align with them in hatred, thereby missing out on not only great maternal love and caring, but the love of childhood friends, grandparents, cousins, aunts, and uncles. This is an unfathomable heartache.

Despite the chasm that exists in my family, somehow, I am blessed with the strength to not be robbed of joy daily. I am grateful that God has given me an amazing ability to move forward and not be stuck in brokenness and despair. Sometimes I wonder why He hasn't intervened or answered my cries, but then I remember that we are all blessed with a free will and make our own choices. My kidss are victimized by Mario's pathogenic parenting choices and lies; it's not their fault. Although that hurts me AND them deeply, my life is good and I choose to be surrounded by friends and loved ones like hot chocolate and warm blankets. A long time ago I learned to make lemonade from lemons, and I happily approach 2017 and look forward to whatever comes my way in the New Year."

Cloaked in year-end prose, I don't think Katy or her friends understood the severity of her situation, nor did her closest friends have the capacity to help her. I think she was desperately reaching for support, yet she was able to say it had been a good year. At the time she didn't understand the cross-generational coalition that all children of alienation are perversely triangulated into, empowering and rewarding them for disrespect, disparagement and detachment from their other parent. From my research and other people's stories, I understand that her kids wanting to show to the world she was the parent who "has a problem" was actually their father using the children to project his perceived self-inadequacies onto Katy. At the time, she had no idea what was happening to her relationship with her kids, but was beginning to recognize what she called a cancer. She truly believed it was a good year, all in all, but was beginning to awaken to the nightmare.

4 PUSH PAST THE BROKEN PIECES
Published in Chicken Soup for the Soul under the title
"Lessons From the Lake"

From a near-death experience at age seven, I acquired the tools to help me overcome my life's greatest challenge 30 years later. Indeed the lessons learned, wisdom gained and tools acquired at such a young age have given me the strength to face many hurdles head-on and have shaped me into who I am.

I grew up next door to the neighborhood playground, which bordered a thick forest surrounding a lake whose body spanned three towns. The woods provided a safe haven to explore nature and enjoy the simple things as I grew through childhood. Wild berries ripened in the Spring sun and they'd burst in my hand sometimes as I picked them from the bushes. With my fingers stained red and my face dripping with juice, I took bucketfuls of blackberries and raspberries home, but could not resist eating the bounty I carried, and rarely had much left over by the time I got to my mother's kitchen. Never quite learning the art of skipping stones on the smooth surface of the lake, wading in shallow coves and canoeing and boating drew me there on summer days. There was a dam at the lake, and when the water was not mightily falling over it, I could walk across it, like a bridge, to pick apples in the town on the other side. On Autumn nights I enjoyed campfires in the woods with my friends, and in the winter we skated on the lake.

In first grade, my best neighborhood friend was a tiny little girl, my age but half my size, named Bobbi. One winter day after a long snowfall, we thought it would be fun to run and slide on the ice in our boots and snow pants. So we walked through the forest in knee-deep snow, marveling at how different our familiar places looked, now dazzled in white. We approached our favorite cove, now covered by a thick blanket of snow, except where the older kids had shoveled an area big enough to play ice hockey. "Out of our way! Go shovel your own snow if you want to play on the ice!" they seemed to say. So, we trudged off toward the middle of the lake hoping to find another place to run and slide.

There is a silence surrounding virgin snow, and it enveloped us as we traversed the frozen lake, far away from the sounds of the older children at play near the shore. After walking a while on the vast expanse of soft, white fluff, we could see what appeared to be a patch of snow-cleared ice to run and slide on! But maybe the ice was so thin there and it was wet on top, maybe the snow had melted as it fell, rather than accumulating on the surface. I feared it would not hold us, but Bobbi had no doubts. Running ahead of me, I can still see her posture as she excitedly kicked the ice with the heel of her boot, beckoning me to come, and hoping to prove the ice was thick and strong enough to hold us both. But it was not.

The surface was paper-thin, and after kicking it, Bobbi immediately fell through. I thought of nothing else but running to her, and I fell in too. Out of earshot from anyone else, we struggled for our lives. Scenes from the movie Titanic captured the chill and shiver of trying to stay alive in frigid water. We were soaked to the skin within seconds, our snow pants and boots heavy, as we treaded violently to keep our heads above the icy water. Attempting to pull ourselves up onto the solid surface of the lake, large pieces of ice broke off and we were submerged again. I knew that crying, whining, and succumbing were not options. No one would hear or see us; we were alone. I tried repeatedly to lift myself out of the icy bath. More pieces would break off, and again I'd push past the broken pieces, but each time I tried to transfer my weight from the water to the surface, the thin ice repeatedly broke and dropped me back into the lake. "Eventually we'll reach thicker ice,",I thought to myself as I struggled to survive. "We're almost there Bobbi, don't give up! Keep trying!" I yelled, not sure if she could hear me, immersed in the sounds of breaking ice and splashing water.

Then from nowhere, three young men appeared. We neither saw nor heard them approach; we just suddenly knew they were there with us. They lay spread-eagle on the ice to distribute their weight, and encouraged Bobbi to grab their single hockey stick as a lifeline. She did, and if they had not pulled her frail little body onto the surface, I don't know how this story would end. At the same time, I continued pushing past broken pieces, and pulled myself up. The three strangers cautioned us not to stand and walk, but advised us to crawl to avoid breaking the thin ice again. Although we didn't understand the physical principles of weight distribution, we heeded their advice and parted company on hands and knees.

After crawling toward shore awhile, I looked over my shoulder in their direction, hoping for a sign it was okay to get off our knees and walk upright again. I have one final image of them in the distance, indelibly etched in my memory. They were skating three abreast toward the town on the other side of the lake, kicking up snow dust behind them and disappearing like angels.

Shivering cold, soaking wet, and turning blue, Bobbi and I approached the cove again, not from the shore this time, but from somewhere beyond the vanishing point in the middle of the lake. The older children were still playing hockey and some stared in disbelief, some didn't even notice, but my older sister laughed hysterically as if we had foolishly played in a puddle and gotten wet. She emoted not a shred of sympathy, just laughter. We tried to tell her what happened to us, but she obviously did not understand we had almost been swallowed by the same lake she was playing on, had almost disappeared forever under the ice.

We trudged onward, out of the woods, growing colder and shivering more violently with every step. Passing the neighborhood playground seemed to take forever, but the warmth of my home was not far away now. Arriving at my house, my mother didn't laugh. She realized by God's grace, our little lives had just been saved. She helped us out of our wet and freezing clothing and submerged us into warm baths. After serving us steaming cupfuls of hot cocoa, she tucked us into bed together, under piles of thick blankets to help keep each other warm. We snuggled together and the shivering eventually stopped. Our body temperatures rose to normal. We recovered, we survived! We bounced back quickly, and soon were looking forward to the wonder and excitement of the next snowfall with childlike anticipation.

Four major lessons emerge when I reflect on what happened that day at the lake. And they continue to guide me and help me through difficult times.

Sometimes in life, you are on thin ice without even knowing. Sometimes, the bottom drops out from under you and you fall. It happened to me when my married life came to a screeching halt. My 19-year marriage had not been a perfect one, but I believed we were attempting to patch things up and move forward in love. Instead, it abruptly ended and more than me, my little children were suffering the emotional carnage of divorce and their dad's hasty remarriage with stepchildren. They needed me to extricate them from the wreckage. My life as full-time mom and primary caregiver was over. I was suddenly a single mom in a new location, working full-time and hoping to re-establish a career. Again I knew crying, whining and feeling sorry for myself were not options. The painful loss of my marriage, redefining myself, rebuilding our family life, restoring my children to wholeness and keeping my head held high was not easy. At times I felt surrounded by the broken pieces of my former life. But I had long before learned how to persevere and keep trying, no matter how many times it takes, or how hopeless it seems. Just like the little girl treading the icy waters, I knew what I needed to do. "Push past the broken pieces and pull yourself up," I told myself, and it is the first of four lessons gleaned from the ice that day.

If help is offered as a lifeline, don't be too proud to accept it. This is the second lesson of the lake. As humbling as it might be, sometimes you cannot succeed alone, and if there are assistance programs or people who want to help, you should graciously accept their kindness. I had left behind a five-bedroom house on two acres adjoining a wildlife preserve, where my son built forts in the woods and we took long meandering walks. But I held my head high as I moved my children into subsidized housing in one of New Jersey's wealthiest towns where I'd found a good job to support them and was later able to purchase a home. Don't be too afraid or too proud to accept help, just as Bobbi grabbed hold of the hockey stick lifeline and was saved.

The third lesson of the lake is sometimes you have to crawl before you can walk again. Starting all over happens one step at a time and cannot be rushed. Like a baby learning to take their first steps, there are lessons to be learned before you stand; before you walk and run. Divorce can put you in a situation that feels as though life has pushed you a few steps backward. It may be tempting to rush things to catch up to where you think you should be. Don't be too quick to spend or borrow money, re-marry or even re-couple. Although you may not understand the greater forces at work, sometimes it's necessary to take your time and crawl before you walk, so the bottom doesn't drop out from under you again.

And finally, piles of thick blankets and hot cocoa were great for defrosting us from the cold that day, and both evoke images of comfort and warmth. The world can be a cold place and the final lesson of the lake is just like hot coca and warm blankets, friends and loved ones can warm you on the inside. As a single person, and the only adult in your household, it's important to keep healthy adult relationships alive. Be in close friendships with kindred souls, so when life gets cold and the world is unkind, you will have a never-ending source of warmth; like hot cocoa and soft, warm blankets.

These are the lessons of the lake, gleaned from the day a trinity of strangers saved Bobbi and me. To this day, no one has ever identified themselves as the heroes of Farrington Lake. No one has come forward to claim honor or receive a medal for saving two little seven year-old girls from an icy death. But the three strangers taught me life's most important lessons and helped me survive divorce and raise three little children on my own. Many, many times over the course of my life have the lessons of the lake helped me carry on and move forward when things seemed bleak and hopeless.

From the trials of our lives there are lessons to be learned, and wisdom to be gained. Pain is not all bad. The break-up of any marriage, other curve balls, even something like falling through the ice, are threads interwoven with love, happiness, fun times, and growth in the tapestry of a person's life. Have faith that each new thread and design brings you closer to the finished fabric of your life, and remember the lessons of the lake as you navigate the precarious footing on your journey, and move forward in life.

Not knowing my children would be alienated from me and all my family members who love them, I was happily moving forward in a positive direction after divorce. I thought the bond between my children and me was invincible.

5 LOVE LETERS WALL

When my second child was born, I received this poem, typewritten on a plain piece of paper tucked in a card welcoming the new baby. Its lyrics had a profound impact on me throughout the lives of all three of my children and remain on my my mind, even now.

A Mother's Prayer, author unknown

I wash the dirt from little feet, and as I wash I pray,
"Lord, keep them ever pure and true, to walk the narrow way."

I wash the dirt from little hands, and earnestly I ask,
"Lord, may they ever yielded beTo do the humblest task."

I wash the dirt from little knees, and pray, "Lord may they be
The place where victories are won, and orders sought from Thee."

I scrub the clothes that soil so soon, and pray, "Lord, may her dress
Through all eternal ages be Thy robe of righteousness."

"Ere many hours shall pass, I know, I'll wash these hands again;
And there'll be dirt upon her dress before the day shall end."

"But as she journeys on through life, and learns of want and pain,
Lord, keep her precious little heart cleansed from all sin and stain."

"For soap and water cannot reach where Thou alone canst see,
Her hands and feet, these I can wash, I trust her heart and soul to thee."

Many years later in the deepest, darkest, lowest point of depression, I was not able to separate the empathetic pain I felt for my children who'd been been told lies and twisted truths, out in the world untethered from their mom (me), from my own pain of losing them. I was feeling that pieces of my heart were also untethered from my soul and being trampled. Like other parents, I considered my pain not as important as the suffering of my children. I reached up out of a pit of darkness and despair, crying out to God through my tears and love rose to the surface like cream on milk. I formed a Facebook group for all parents of lost children to express LOVE to them, even though their children may never see or read it. The following is excepted from the introduction to the Love Letters Wall group page. The name was later changed to Letters and Happy Birthdays to Lost Children.

"Like an old stone wall with letters tucked between the rocks in the hopes someone will read them some day, this wall is a quiet place. It is built with love. A place for parents to share "I Love You" to their children who cannot hear because they have been taught to hate them. It's a place to forget about the ex, forget about court, forget about what makes you mad, and just say I love you in any way you can. Maybe someday, some child will find these notes and turn their hearts toward a parent pushed out of their life.

This group was created to give wounded parents a safe place, a metaphoric wall, to write positive, encouraging letters to the children we love and will always love. By participating and sharing your thoughts in a safe place they won't be 'returned-to-sender' or deleted unread, and it is hoped you will write to them giving voice and expression to your love. By writing, you will also bring solace to others who read your words and are comforted knowing they are not alone in their pain. And who knows? Maybe someday, some way, an alienated child will stumble upon the wall and be reminded there is a parent out there who loves them, and it's time for them to come home emotionally. So think about joining and contributing to Letters and Happy Birthdays to Lost Children. It's for you. It's for your children. It's for all of us."

In the following letters, names have been changed to protect and respect the privacy of individuals.

June 2010
Dear Timothy,

One of the hardest things in the world I had to do was walk away when the music played and parents and families stormed the field to meet their graduating seniors for hugs and kisses and pictures. I wanted so much to be a part of that happiness with you, Nate, Adam, Patrick, and so many of your friends I know and who have come on vacation with us, slept over, and had so many meals together with. But out of respect for you, I walked away. You later texted I ruined your day because somehow you knew I was there. I pray for wisdom and guidance all the time and hope God will turn your heart toward me again. I remember walking into the grocery store the day before Father's Day and you just happened to be walking out at that moment. "Hi Timothy!" I said, and you just gave me an angry look. I am so sorry it's like this. I see you run in the other direction when I go to Walmart and I feel bad, for you obviously have unwarranted fear. I have never bothered you at work, nor do I ever intend to interfere. It's as if you are under some type of spell telling you to hate me. I just don't get it. I want my sweet spirited son to reemerge. I deserve a relationship with you. Love, Dad

October 2010
Dear Amy,

    I guess you are doing fine, and I will always be proud of your independence, strength, intelligence, and kindness to others.

    I wish you could see the progress your Uncle Tim is making on the upstairs renovation. In six weeks, Jennifer's and your bedrooms will be finished, a new bathroom, and a small den/study. It's exciting to see the transformation taking shape, you are welcome to stop by and see it!

    I am and will always be sorry for mistakes I made that caused you to feel hurt. I wish I could erase anything I've ever said or done wrong and leave you with only the happy, loving sweet memories of times together. I wanted to be a perfect mom but I know that's an impossible feat. I wanted to give you an enriching childhood with arts-n-crafts projects together, bed-time stories, trips to farms, homemade meals, breads and ice cream, cuddling on the couch before school, coaching you in sports, exposing you to gymnastics and other indoor sports, beach day trips, family vacations, etc.

    I wanted you to know your feelings and emotions were important and what's inside you is just as valid and important as what's on the outside. When you cried, I encouraged you to cry out all the frustration, confusion and pain. "Let it all out," I would say. "Cry out all the bad stuff". I would hurt too, when you hurt. And I was happy when you were happy; that's just a normal parent trait.

    For all these reasons I am so sad and sorry for mistakes I made along the way you cannot forget.

Sorry I've hurt you, when I have always loved you so, so much. "Her name is Amy Paulette, and she will change my life forever," I wrote in my diary when you were born. And you did change me. You made me a stronger, better mother and person in so many ways. I always wanted you to be safe from hurt, and since the day you were born I've always prayed, "Lord please keep her safe from injury, illness, or harm". It has been my prayer for all of you, and still is to this day.

I hope you will soon be ready to forgive me. It's never too late to come home and start over. You have a loving home and family here and in a few weeks a nice, new bedroom and bathroom too. Love, Mom

November 2012
Dear Dan and Isabelle,

Happy Thanksgiving! I am thankful for the love we shared and the bond we had, and joy and privilege I had of raising you. Miss you and love you forever... Love, Daddy

August 2013
Dear Amy and Jennifer,

There is so much I want to say to you and some of it may not be right for "Love Letters Wall", but some may. Mostly, I want to tell you it's not your fault. You can always turn your heart toward home; toward me. My heart is waiting for you.

Amy, I found a six year old child's drawing of a mother driving to work. Above her head was a thought bubble. Inside the bubble was a drawing of a little girl and inside her thought bubble were the words "I love you mom". You drew that. You knew I thought of you every minute we were apart. You knew I loved you. I hung that drawing above my desk at work for a long time. I hold images like that in my heart forever.

Jennifer, another memory is of us... You had already started to say hurtful things to me, and about me, things a part of you knew were not true. But when your teenaged boyfriend broke up with you after persuading you to something you didn't want to, you turned to me. I held you close while you sobbed and told you it's ok, and you're going to be ok. I told you I would go pick him up by his privates, swing him around over my head and throw him far, far away. We laughed through tears, knowing I couldn't and wouldn't do that and never had a violent bone in my body. But we both knew how fiercely protective I was of your feelings and your heart. And like many other times, when your sister came home, I asked her to go sit with you and put her arm around you.

It has always and will continue to always sadden me you were taught I was no good and from an early age taught to be ashamed of your love for your mother. You began to say that you never want to speak to me or see me again as soon as you are legally able to leave our home. And although you were vulnerable and unprepared to sustain yourself for the rest of your life, you did leave. You worked lots of a part-time hours, and you went to college and you severed your relationship with me, and your life became even harder than it had to be. My world fell apart, but I stooped and built it up again with worn out tools, and created something different from the rubble. It's basically a happy life and a good life, but a piece of my heart has been amputated, and the pain I live with daily is not phantom pain. It's real; a piece of my heart really is out there in the world untethered and being stomped upon by people who hurt you, and thus hurt me too.

I know your path isn't easy. I know it's hard for you to think of me at all; the happy memories of closeness, knowing you always had an advocate in your corner at all times, the bonds of love, the baking, sewing, crafts, the wisdom, advice and love have all been obscured by the hatred, disgust and disregard you were induced to feel.

Sadly, it's made you feel like there's something wrong with you too. You don't like yourself or your situation very much, something cannot admit that. You are confused, you are hurting and you feel all alone; it's immensely painful for you and fraught with shame, guilt and disorientation, but you stuff this feelings deep down inside. It's not your fault and there's a way to be free of the pain caused by all of that. There is a way to make it right again; there is a way to start over. I know it can't be easy for you, but I pray every day your heart will be turned once again toward mommy who has always loved you. Love, Mommy

August 2013
Dear Thomas and Gina,

Every night I say a prayer that you are okay, happy and strong. I pray that if you're not, God will bless and comfort you each and every day. I know you wish I didn't think about you and probably wish I didn't pray for you. But when I lay my head on my pillow I do.

Before he died, Grandpa told me every night he prayed with Grandma for all their children and grandchildren - and that included you and me. It's the natural thing to do. When you have children, you'll find it natural to do the same.

I'm so sorry for you and me for the pain, injury and harm that came. I hope and believe the love coming your way from me - that was always coming your way - has given you strength to get through life with all the confusing, crazy mixed up feelings you have toward me and the family. But please don't hate or blame yourselves. You are good; you always were. There is a way to make things right again; I pray you find the way and walk in the path that will lead to healing. Love, Mom

October 2013
Dear Sherry,

Congratulations on making the dean's list. I know... I'm a little late... a lot late... it takes me a while to hear about you. But, I am still very proud of all your years on the high school honor roll, and like I told you when you were little, you'd be accepted to every college you applied for, time proved that to be true! University Junior and Senior now, I am sure you are doing great and many doors will continue to open for you. Remain strong through everything life sends your way. It's been years now since we've spoken, and I know alienation from a parent whom you once had a normal, healthy, loving bond with is painful on the inside, even when the emotions are buried very deep. I hadn't believed this could happen to us, and it took me a long time to accept it did. Just remember, no matter where you are, no matter where I am, you can always come home. The bonds of love that unite us have not been broken here; they are still very strong and my heart is waiting for your heart. I love you always and in all ways. Love, Dad

November 2013
Dear Joey and Greg,

When I lay my head on my pillow each night I think of you and what has happened. Actually, I think of you many times during the day as well. Please don't ever forget the laughter, the closeness, the bond we shared. There's a way to make things right again. I miss you so much and want you in my life. It's not the same without you. It never will be. Love, Mama

November 2013
Dear Thomas and Gina,

When I grocery shop and when I cook, I remember and still look for the foods you liked and want to make them for you, then before reaching for them on the store shelf, I remember you are gone. When I prepare for holidays, I imagine your faces around the table and I want you there, with your brother, your Grandma, aunts, uncles, and cousins. When I paint and create art I remember your creativity and talent. I think of the smiles and laughter of our stable, happy, home life. I remember being your strongest advocate when life treated you unfairly. I tried to provide all the best opportunities for you to grow to be the best individuals you could be.

You were very different from each other, and it was evident from the moments I first held you. I wanted to give you opportunities to reach your full potentials. I parented with purpose, very deliberate about raising you with strong roots and strong wings to be independent, emotionally secure, young women, and I believe you did become that. I am able to look at myself in the mirror every day and know although I made mistakes like all parents do along the way, I did the best I could. I miss you and wish we could have the relationship we are supposed to have as your birthdays approach. I know the world can be a cold, cold place, and I hope you surround yourselves with good friends and loved ones like hot chocolate and warm blankets. Mostly I hope your hearts come home, where they belong. Love, Mom

December 2013
My Darlings,
   Of course as the holidays approach and your birthday months are here I am full of thoughts of you. I hope you have sweet memories of our holiday baking together and making candles, soaps, and gifts of food for your friends and teachers. I love you, miss you and wish you both happy birthdays and warm cozy Christmases, wherever you are. Love, Daddy

December 2013
Dear Billy
   Thinking of you and hoping you had a good Christmas. I just want you to know, no matter how long it takes, no matter where you live or

how far, I will always be ready to work with you on fixing our relationship. Whenever you are ready, know that I am too. Merry Christmas. Love, Dad

December 2013
Dear John,

Thank you for stopping by yesterday. I'm glad you got to see and hug and talk to some of your overseas cousins, aunts and uncles. If you stayed longer you would have seen your brother too, and Uncle Ralph's baby twins are now six-year old young ladies! You look well and I am still proud of how you've grown up. I understand you had to pretend I was completely invisible to you and not acknowledge. It's okay, but it hurts like hell. I hope you opened the presents I gave you and didn't throw them away, but I really don't know if you want my gifts. I made the necklace out of a cut stone I thought you'd love. Do what you have to do, as you allow yourself to begin to feel the love of this side of your family which has never diminished. We all love you as much as ever. Love, Papa

February 2014
Dear Amy My Angel and Jenny Belle,

Yesterday was my birthday and tomorrow is my shoulder surgery. I thought a lot about the mother I had and the mother I am. I was roasting chicken and potatoes the way Grandma had done and the house smelled like hers. Without her specifically teaching me, I learned to cook well just by observation. It was a good feeling to reflect on the similarities between my mom and me. I thought of both of you and wished you could have the same good feeling. We are so much alike and someday I hope you will rejoice in that. I had a great birthday with friends and only wished you were there also. Tomorrow after my surgery I will be helped by friends and loved ones too. I think of you lots, and hope you got the Valentine's Day flowers I sent. Love, Mommy

March 2014
Dear Jack and Tara,
May the God of hope fill you with all joy and peace as you trust in him, so that you may overflow with hope by the power of the Holy Spirit. — Romans 15:13. Love, Pop

April 2014
Dear Alex,
I love you as much as I ever did and I miss you! I know the chasm between us can be lessened and we can have a loving, healthy, caring relationship once again. That's my wish and that's my impossible dream I dare to dream. Love, Dad

Mother's Day Letter 2014
Dear Amy and Jennifer,
Do you remember when you and your brother all camped out on the floor of my bedroom at the old house? When you wanted to camp out in the Family Room, I slept down there with you. With summer coming, I can see me shaking sand off the beach blanket and letting the wind raise it like a sail as I held the corners. You both liked running under it before it floated back down to the sand. I did a similar thing when I tucked you

in at night and a gentle puff of my love breezed over you.

Do you remember me holding you when you cried, or stroking your back when you got older, and telling you to go ahead and cry out all the hurt and pain? I told you crying lets all the bad stuff come out. Do you remember the songs we sang to your baby dolls as we held and rocked them? Later, we sang those same songs to your baby cousins and the newborns of my friends. Do you remember helping me quilt blankets for them, and then cutting up favorite clothes you grew out of to make clothes and blankets for your dolls? I do.

A friend posted a picture of a box turtle they saved from certain death on the road. It sparked memories of the pond turtles we saved in cardboard boxes with grass and leaves, and let go after one day of gentle captivity. Do you remember the one that seemed frantic to get out of the box, so we let her out in our garden and watched in awe as she dug a hole and lay an egg? Do you remember how the Baltimore Oriel nest was woven like a burlap sack and hung in our tree? Do you remember the Spring when a pair of fawns came regularly to the property, and I brought you to the window to see them? We called them our "pet deer" and named them Spotty and Dotty. Yes, they were eating my flowers, but I cherished the opportunity to teach you about wildlife when we quietly went to the window and observed them in silence.

When I make soaps, candles, and food for friends I wonder if you remember all the home-crafted gifts we made for your friends and teachers. The years we made fragrant soaps; do you remember we also made beautiful velvet sacks with gold ribbon drawstrings to package them? Muddy Buddies in mason jars, or holiday mugs, was a gift you continued to give friends all the way into your high school years. I watched you transform from little children to confident generous souls as you began to make gifts of food by yourselves for friends who were lonely or hurting.

Like all moms, I reflect back on the precious time I had to raise you to be the best, most complete people you could be. Deep roots and very strong wings are what I wanted to give you. But I never could have dreamed in my worst nightmare that you'd fly so prematurely, with such contempt and disdain for the nest from which you came. It's not your fault, and I know you love me and I hope there is a memory of my love inside you too. I remember it all; all the time. Do you? Love, Mommy

May 2014
Dear Jack and Tara,

My prayer for all of us comes from the book of Romans: "May the God who gives endurance and encouragement give us a spirit of unity among ourselves as we follow Christ Jesus, so that with one heart and mouth we may glorify the God and Father of our Lord Jesus Christ." - Romans 15:5-6

I love you always and all ways and it will never change. Please turn your hearts toward me. Love, Pop

May 2014

I think you know the wisdom I have always shared with you is mostly from God's word, the Bible. One of the things I tried to do, although it may not have seemed that way from a child's perspective, was maintain a drama-free life and household. It's summed up in the following verse and another of my prayers for all of us.... "My dear brothers, take note of this: Everyone should be quick to listen, slow to speak and slow to become angry." — James 1:19

August 2014

Dear Jessie and Adam,

Even on my happiest days, there is a sadness within. It's normal for a parent's happiness to be partially tied in some way to their relationships with their children. Just like it's normal for children's (even adult children's) happiness to be tied to their healthy relationship with their mother. I have a gift of inner strength that keeps me afloat and allows me to experience joy, happiness, growth and forward momentum that can't be stopped, and ironically, I hope I have bestowed that gift upon you. For what you go through, hating (me) your father, and wanting to be nothing like him, have nothing to do with him, believing he needs to be punished, you need this gift too. Yes, I have a few very sad days, where tears flow at a simple memory of joy we shared, or lessons we learned together, or experiences, or belly laughter where we couldn't stop. Yes, I endure entire days on the verge of tears. But there are 365 days each year and most of those days are good, rich, and fulfilling. I wish the same for you.

But mostly I wish you will feel empowered to turn your heart toward your biggest advocate who loves you in the most sacrificial way. It's scary, I know. You don't even know how or what to say; I understand that. But I hope the day comes soon when you are ready to take a baby step toward me, and I will be there with open arms (and fatted calf, if you understand that metaphor). I love you and wish you all the good things life can give you. Love, Daddy

August 2014
Dear Joey and Greg,
I think of you when I hear this song…
"Who You Are Today" (Kenny Chesney; I slightly changed lyrics)

Sunny days seem to hurt the most. I wear the pain like a heavy coat.
I feel you everywhere I go.
I see your smile, I see your face, I hear you laughin' in the rain.
I still can't believe you're gone.

It ain't fair: you left too young, like a story that had just begun,
But hate tore the pages all away.
God knows how I miss you, all the pain that I go through,
Just knowin' no one could take your place.
An' sometimes I wonder, who you are today.

Have you seen the world? Have you chased your dreams?
Do you sometimes miss our family?

I wonder what would you name your babies?
Some days the sky's so blue, I feel that I could talk to you,
An' I know it might sound crazy.

It ain't fair: you left too young, like a story that had just begun,
But hate tore the pages all away.
God knows how I miss you, all the pain that I go through,
Just knowin' no one could take your place.
An' sometimes I wonder, who you are today.

Sunny days seem to hurt the most. I wear the pain like a heavy coat.
The only thing that gives me hope, is I know I'll see you again some day.
Some day, some day, some day.

September 2014
To Tom, John, and Sophia,

That's me at four or five years old, on the swing in the orange bathing suit and that's Uncle Jigs who comes to sit with me. Aunt Diane is in the pink dress and beautiful Grandma in the gold dress. Grandpa's obvious; he's the one joking around with everyone. The blond boys are Uncles Tommy, Peter and Richard. The dark-haired haired men are Grandpa's brothers and nephews; my uncles and cousins. You might recognize Uncle Sardi dancing. The oldest woman is Grandpa's mom: my Gramma, your great-grandmother. We were celebrating her birthday. The backyard fence is still there, you may even remember it in Gramma and Grandpa's backyard.

The video is a warm reminder to us all of where we came from. May you never forget the love of your family. It's generational. Love always, Papa

September 2014
Dear Michael,
 I write metaphorically to you on this FB page hoping it will reach someone someday. Hoping it will bring reconciliation to some deserving souls. Hoping and knowing it brings a certain solace to others to read and know they are not alone in their pain and abandonment. But I dare not ever hope one of you, my loves, will read it. Never do I believe that. Because hoping and believing that would bring an expectation with it. An unmet expectation. But I do wonder what I really would say if I really, really could write you. It almost scares me to not know if my letter would enrage you or bring a smile. That is scary and I know it would be just as scary for you to try to reach out after all this time. Sometimes we all choose the less scary route, don't we?
 That's a sad thing though. Sometimes the scary route leads to self-discovery, truth, and new beginnings in peace. So far, that's all I know; it's scary. I don't know if you want to hear I am very proud of you and although a terrible chasm is between us which hurts me and damages you, I think of you all the time and desire a normal relationship, untainted, unblemished by opinions of others. Do you really want to hear that, or does it make you cringe? I'm sure even in the best scenario it must produce some discomfort and disquiet in your soul.
 Would I ask if you understand your dismissal

of a parent, and why it's unhealthy to try to make the once loving bond vanish completely? I really don't know if you would just be creeped out and continue to believe the lies and I wonder if you'd wish things remained as they are now and I could not ever reach you? Would you be taken aback if I really sent you a letter? These are the thoughts of parents whose children have been taught to hate. They wonder if their child would be antagonized by their words of love and pride. No other parents would ever, ever question whether their children would wish they weren't loved by their parent and wish it was never expressed. I really don't know what I would say if I actually could reach you. I just know it's a little scary. Love and miss you, Daddy

November 2014
Dear Amy and Jennifer,

I was thinking today about the hopes I had when I bought the house in 2008.

It was the second real estate closing I'd participated in as a single mom. The first was when I bought the condominium from a young couple having a child who needed something "bigger, with more space", a feeling I understood, having once been in their situation and purchased a five bedroom house which became our family home for 11 years. Yet with two growing daughters and a teenaged son who visited frequently I was there buying the only thing I could afford in Warwick, NJ; a two bedroom condominium deemed too small for a couple expecting one child. I wasn't happy about it, but my mortgage payment would be less than the rent

I'd been paying the past two years for a three bedroom rental, and it would hopefully propel me to buy something more appropriate in time. Seven years later, I was the one selling the 2-bedroom condo, and I sat alone at the closing with no one there to celebrate.

Across the table from me sat the buyer, flanked by her fiancé, father and mother; lovely people, all of them. As I signed my name multiple times, the contrast hit me. They were so happy, so grateful to find such a decent place, so eager to celebrate the moment with her and excited to fix it up and move her in! I had made improvements while there. I'd replaced worn out carpeting with wood flooring, installed a dishwasher, new refrigerator and new stove. But we'd lived hard in too-small space, and it needed a facelift. Their purchase, and mine seven years before, had represented very different things. Of course, I now had the hindsight of some very difficult years there. They had the hope of new beginnings.

And then my third closing, where I was the one with hope. I'd wished I'd had a partner by my side to say "Honey we did it! We bought a house!" I really, really wished for that, but at least I had the pride I was providing a place for you both to have more privacy and room to finish growing up. The first set of renovations included a 500-square foot deck so I could provide the much-missed outdoor living space we lost in the condominium. I also built a fire pit at ground level and L-shaped benches on the upper level for you and your friends, indeed we had many BBQs and parties there! But mostly I'd hoped that you'd become happier with more elbow room now. I set up well-stocked study tables in the basement, two couches, a TV and a table for puzzles; the first puzzle we worked on together was Charlie Brown, and thanks to Amy's dedication, completed it quickly! I thought the hardest years were over because I believed much of your anger was due to cramped quarters, while your dad still had the five bedroom house we had purchased together. I was looking forward to the growing-up of my daughters, prom pictures, college trips. I taught you to drive cars, and I gave you more and more independence and responsibility with the passage of time. And it was much too late when I learned the hardest times were still ahead.

For at the house on Westfield, some days my dreams came true. I was grateful I could provide what I thought you needed, and within two years, I added a bathroom for you and two larger bedrooms. You attended church with me on Sundays again and brought your friends. In high school you were honor students, worked part-time and competed on teams. But the good days were becoming fewer and farther between the days when, completely unprovoked, you threatened your plans. "I'm leaving home the day I turn 18 and you will never see me again!" a pact made when you may have been too young to remember. You only knew you HAD to do it, to prove your final loyalty to the coalition you were triangulated into against your will. My new normal was not knowing why, when, or how quickly you could become angry with no justification, and start spewing insults at me I'd previously heard only from your father. It was as if you were his marionettes, with him pulling the strings. No boss, nor friend, nor enemy, nor brother or sister, nor therapist ever used those adjectives (psycho, lazy, fake, phony, no-good, worthless, unchristian) to describe me. I'd only heard them from one man, who projected his own self-loathing on to me, and accused me of everything he hated in his own character. Then I began hearing it from you, my sweet my daughters with whom I'd once had a close, healthy, loving bond. Angry outbursts and lashing out at me became more frequent and built to a crescendo until the days you left. I am sure it helped you break away from my love's reach, to hate me more passionately.

Another thing happened during those same years. I had the blessing of helping Tyler crawl out of rock bottom and set his mind toward recovery. The house on Westfield meant when Tyler's apartment flooded, and he had to move out, I could welcome him to set up a basement apartment in our home. Our relationship was restored and we began to become close again as he grew into a man on my watch. I had new opportunities to mother him, to teach him to tie a tie and wear a tuxedo, and get him started with his driver's license, a car and see him fall in love and get married. We learned together about butchering and cooking venison when he taught himself to hunt and field dress deer. And without him, I don't know how I could have endured your rejection. His love and affection got me through those years. When he was ready to go across the country to set up home in California, I gave him my blessing and told him the past six years had been the BEST! and I meant it. But they were the worst years too because I lost you my daughters, and he lost his sisters. I understand why, but I wish you did not have to reject him too. He needs his sisters, just like I need my daughters. Love, Mom

November 2014
Dear Amy and Jennifer,
Wow, these last few months have seen some real physical changes making me feel old. I imagine if you saw me now, you'd notice I'm no longer the "unstoppable, able to make anything, able to fix everything, killer of stink bugs and spiders kinda mom" you might remember. But I am fixing what can be fixed on my body, one step at a time, starting last winter with my shoulder and biceps surgery. In the past few months I have had several flare-ups of my collapsing spine; one almost paralyzed me in bed for an entire day. So, trying a few non-surgical remedies, but talking about spinal revision surgeries. I cannot allow my skeletal system to remain on the trajectory it's on now; it's absolutely unsustainable. I thought I'd have a few more months at least, before an intervention would be needed. I think about you both so much and hope you have continued to have your own backs checked and you'll never need scoliosis surgery, but if you do, the procedures in place today have changed so much to prevent the "later in life" degeneration and spinal collapse. I hope you never feel the pain I feel. Love always, Mom

November 2014
Dear Jess,
"...I have not stopped praying for you and asking God to fill you with the knowledge of his will through all spiritual wisdom and understanding." — Colossians 1:9

Black Friday 2014
Another holiday passed without you. I served eighteen of your Aunts, Uncles, and cousins for a sit down dinner. You would have loved it here. I was so happy to have so much love in our home. It was a wonderful day of family and guitar playing from 2:00 pm until almost midnight. But today I reflect on what was missing - YOU!

December 2014
I don't know what to say, so I can only imagine you don't know what to say either. Not a day goes by I don't lay my head on my pillow and think of you. We had a close, healthy, loving bond. We had fun. We enjoyed each other's company. I want that back. Do you? I miss you so much it hurts like an open wound. Love, Dad

December 2014, Dear Christopher and Kara,
I love you. I miss you. Please come home for Christmas in your hearts.

January 2015, Rachel and Jen,
Come home my darlings. I'm coping and living a full life, with surprising joy, but NOTHING compares to you. Come back please... in your hearts... please turn your hearts toward home; toward me. Love, Dad

January 2015
So many things trigger memories of happy times together and I keep wondering when you will realize I am a normal, happy, person who loves God and loves you in the most natural, healthy way. You are my children and I miss you so much. I keep wondering and waiting for your return. But I have a full, busy and miraculously happy life. It's just this big, gaping emotional wound will not heal. Come back home in your hearts. Please come back to me my darlings. Love, Pop

February 2015
To my stars, Johnny and Tess,
I was listening to some old Glen Campbell music Grandma and Grandpa used to like and I came across this. I remember appreciating the lyrics and metaphor with it when I was a child. I don't know why I identified with it then, but I do now too. It's all about my love for you my stars, and trying my hardest to change what I cannot change, and so I changed the words a bit. I miss you so much!

My Dream (aka Impossible Dream - I changed some lyrics)

To dream the impossible dream, to fight the unbeatable foe
To bear with unbearable sorrow, to run where the brave dare not go

To right the unrightable wrong, to love pure and chaste from afar
To try when your arms are too weary, to reach the unreachable star

This is my quest, to follow that star
No matter how hopeless, no matter how far

To fight for the right, without question or pause
To be willing to march into Hell, for a heavenly cause

And I know if I'll only be true, to this glorious quest
That my heart will lie peaceful and calm, when I'm laid to my rest

And my kids will be better for this, that I, scorned and covered with scars
Still strove with my last ounce of courage, to reach the unreachable star.

February 2015
My Darling Daughter,
    Valentine's Day is coming and I wish I knew where to send you something. In the years when I knew where, I sent flowers to you both at your places of employment. I never knew if you threw them directly into the trash, but I guessed there might have been Valentine's Days no one acknowledged their love for you except for me and the flowers I sent. I want to do this again. I want to do it every birthday and every Christmas and every Valentine's Day. I want you to know you are thought of, you are valued, you are

wonderful, you are my daughters. I know you may never stumble upon this wall and read these letters tucked away for you, but I hope something inside you remembers and knows we are family; we are one and will always be part of each other. I am a good part of you, and you of me, and it would be healthy for you to embrace that some day. I am so sorry it got all twisted up for you. We are missing out on the best parts of life on this earth. You cannot imagine that's true, but you will someday. I hope it's soon. there's a funny thing about hope; it really does spring eternal in the human breast, no matter the circumstances. You're getting older now and I know it's scary to try to sort things out, but when you take that step to rediscover us, I will be there for you. I love you and always will. Love, Daddy

October 2015
Dear Rachel and Jen,

It isn't normal to hate a good parent. Few people understand what happened in our once loving relationship with normal, close, loving bonds. Few people understand how hard it would be for you to abandon your indoctrination, and see once again the real me, and who and what I am. No one knows why you would cling to an irrational hatred and belief that I am only fooling people who know me as a kind, giving, thoughtful, empathetic, normal, Christian person. Most folks have no idea what makes a child hate a parent so much. It is not normal to sever the parent-child bond. No one understands why I am not angry. I am so, so, so sad this happened, but I think I understand all of it. I still cry some days when I think of you and all the wonderful, loving times, and the normal, healthy, loving bond we had as I raised you with deep roots and strong wings to fly and find your separate identities in life. I think there will always be sporadic days I will cry, as long as you keep yourselves apart from me with no way to communicate. I am and will always be sad you've had to separate yourselves from so many people who love you; cousins, aunts, uncles, Grandma, even many of your old friends. But I will never let sadness and loss define me. I do not live as a victim, but a survivor, no matter what curve ball life throws, and I taught you to live that way too! I am so sorry you were made to feel you had to make a choice to love only one parent and hate the other. I remember telling you in your angry adolescent times, "No matter how strong your anger and hatred is, my love for you will always be stronger." I hope deep down inside you always remember and believe that. I hope someday you will abandon your adolescent beliefs and behaviors, and find only grace, forgiveness, and love from me at the end of the irrational hatred you've taken into adulthood. Love, Dad

December 2015
Adam,
    About 18 years ago I held you in my arms as you sobbed "It's not fair! Divorce isn't fair!" You had just returned from a weekend visit to Dad's and step-family. You felt it so deeply, yet you were only six. All I could say was "I know honey, it's not fair", as I stroked your hair. I knew divorce wasn't fair to kids, and I always wanted you to feel

safe to express all your feelings, because I knew that was very healthy. I had no idea what happened or what was said at dad's house to make you burst into tears, but I held you until the hurt went away.

Brooke, when you were seven, you came home from dad's sobbing, "I don't think he loves me!" I held you tight and assured you he did. "He loves you, I know he does." Inside I was hurting so much for you that he would make you feel unloved. I knew things that would be wrong to tell you, so I held me tongue. I believed everyone needs a relationship with both parents, so I encouraged you to believe he was good and loving.

To you both: I did not know he was afraid. Afraid of losing you, as if in a competition where he had to be the winner, not the loser. He was so afraid you would not love him unless he could make you hate me and believe you don't need your mother, and cut off all the people who know and like me. And then, when he severed the normal, healthy, loving bond with me and all your family on this side, he believed he could then rest secure knowing he was loved and would not be abandoned by you. I knew how he did that to me in the marriage (isolated me from my family and friends), but I didn't know he could or would do that to his kids.

I AM SO SORRY I DIDN'T KNOW HE WAS ABUSING YOU IN THIS WAY. I AM SO SORRY FOR ANYTHING I DID TO HURT YOU. Normal people do NOT persuade kids to un-love their parent and entire side of their family. You were both right... that's not love, and it's not fair. Love, Mum

January 2016
Happy Birthday Jennifer,
   I found these diary entries from the day you were born, and about a week later, 23 years ago. I was so in love with you and still am! You've grown up to be a smart strong woman with strong wings to fly, just as I hoped you would. I wish you every happiness and ask only that you please come home in your heart.
   "Saturday, January 16, 1993 - It's 9:00 right now. Jennifer was born at 7:29 a.m., weighing 7 pounds, 8 ounces. It's now 11:35 a.m. I've already eaten breakfast and lunch and ready to doze. Jennifer is beside me in her clear plastic isolette. I was just watching her lay there and thinking of the miracle that just yesterday, just this morning, she was inside me instead. Just as alive, just as much of a person but inside me alive. Now outside me alive.
   Thank you Lord that she's so healthy. Thank you that I made it through with no anesthesia, no medication, no episiotomy. Thank you for another wonderful life to nurture. Help me to be the best I can be for her and my others. She lifts her head real well. She's going to be strong like Tyler and Amy.
   …I was holding Jenifer and she was quiet and alert and looking around, and I thought this is what I love about not being medicated for their birth. It's a nice feeling to be awake with my baby, while she is so alert.That's the part I like so much. So I decided to savor every moment here and now, and just drink her in. To absorb her. I

stared, quiet and alert also. Quiet precious moments with my newborn baby. I loved it and hope I will never forget this.

…(about a week later) Jennifer is so special. I think I love her even more because she needs me in a special way. She needs to be held more, fed more, than my other children. She seems to be in discomfort much of the time with her sweet little face all wrinkled up and her loud crying. It just makes me want her more. I feel an immediate, strong maternal infant bond more urgently than I remember feeling before. I want to change her mind, coax her out of her discomfort, teach her that her new world is comfortable, her world is a loving place where people care, where I care about her, about her needs, a place where she'll always be cared for. I want to give that to her; that secure feeling that she doesn't need to cry so hard. That it's okay. That everything will be okay."

February 2016
To Tom, John, Sophia,

FORGIVENESS: To all children who were ever caught in the alienation trap, and taught shame, hate, blame, and harbor only bitterness toward one parent and all members of "that side" of the family: It's not your fault and we don't blame you. We know it's not natural for a child to irrationally hate their parent (or anyone) with whom you had a normal, healthy, loving bond. If you are a grown-up now, you know it's true too; you know it's not normal to feel the way you do. You know it's not normal to be ashamed of loving your family. We understand it hurts to ask yourself why you feel this way. We just want healing for your brain-raped mind and soul. We know it's much easier to avoid your childhood friends who still love and adore your mom or dad, to avoid cousins, aunts, uncles, and grandparents who love you. It's less painful to stay in the lies you were taught. We understand the cognitive dissonance you feel if you enter the company of normal people who feel good about your mom or dad. It's so strong that you've had to avoid and discard all of those good people in your life. It's not easy for you to look at or even think about what went wrong, why you ever wanted to detach from so much love coming your way, and it's hard to erase all good, happy, loving memories by replacing them with lies you were told. But now grown up, you do wonder about it sometimes. You try not to think about it, but you do sometimes, because it's healthy and natural to think about those who always had your back and whose love is everlasting. It takes great maturity and real courage to do that because it's very scary now. Facing your own personal truth will hurt on so many levels as you regret the words you've said and the behaviors you've exhibited without provocation. It will cast doubts and aspersions upon the people who taught you to think and feel this way and you will feel frightened and uncomfortable. Please don't be afraid. Don't be ashamed. You are forgiven for the hurt and pain and we don't need to bring it up. We will not ask you to defend or discuss it. We only ask your forgiveness for our mistakes and any hurt and/or pain we caused because we always loved you so much. When you forgive yourself and forgive us for hurtful mistakes or confusing you further, then your healing can begin. We want you to be whole, healed, healthy and happy. You really can't be all that when you've thrown away relationships with normal, healthy, family members and others people who always loved you, still love you and will love you forever. We offer forgiveness, love and respect. We yearn for the same in return so your journey to wholeness can begin. Love Papa (and all the parents…)

June 2016
Brooke and Adam,

So sorry you missed Grandmother's funeral. I think something every human should do is attend the funeral of their grandparents. Or at least send condolences in some way. It's sad to see you either weren't notified of her death or chose to not reach out to this side of your family in response. I'd prefer to believe you weren't notified. Lots of love is still coming your way in the form of, "How are Brook and Adam?" everywhere I go. You are adults now and a part of me is with you and always will be, but the choice is yours to keep running and hiding from your mum who has always, and will always love you. The rest of your family and friends want you in their lives too. I know it's scary to remove yourself from the course you are on, avoiding all this love that could be in your lives, but you are the ones who must open the door, even just a crack. No one can open that door for you. But we can keep loving you - and we do! It's your turn now to let go of childish decisions you made when you were immature and easily swayed, and not fear the love, but receive all the good things God has given you

- not to just pick and choose, but accept every good thing and person, and we pray that you soon will love again without fear. Love, Mum

November 2016
To my kids and all lost children,
   This group is about writing to you, our lost children. Not because we believe you will read the letters, but because we need to express our love. That's a natural human need and without you in our lives, we don't really have an outlet to express it in normal ways so we come here. I've said a lot to you over the years about my open door, arms, and heart, and hoping you would turn toward the love of your mother once again. I forgive you for the path I understand you felt you had to take. But it doesn't really get easier for me with time. As the years go by and the chasm gets wider, it hurts more and more. My prayer and hope is you will remember being loved, and feeling loved, and the many ways I demonstrated love for you. And I hope and pray the meditations of your hearts and words of your mouths, and the thoughts in your heads will be pleasing to God. That you will be holy and be strengthened with power through His spirit so that Christ may dwell in your hearts through faith; and that you, being rooted and grounded in love, may be able to comprehend the breadth and length and height and depth, and to know the love of Christ which surpasses knowledge, that you may be filled up to all the fullness of God. That's my prayer. AMEN! Love, Daddy

6 BUBBLEGUM IN THE TANK
Originally published in The Showcase Magazine

I'd noticed the floor had been perpetually damp behind the toilet. Investigating, I discovered there was a slow leak from the underside of the tank. I put a bucket under it to catch the dripping, and made a mental note to call the plumber. A few days went by, but I felt no sense of urgency because it took an entire day for the bucket to fill, and then I'd empty it in the bathtub and start again. In the divorce aftermath, I'd learned some quick fixes around the house. Still, there were times when I really needed to hire a professional.

Two days later I was getting ready to pick up my daughter from day camp, when the bucket began rapidly overflowing. Throwing towels on the floor to catch the torrent, I dumped the bucket into the tub, discovering the bolt which connects the tank to the toilet bowl had rusted right through and landed in the bucket. Now, through the large hole in the bottom of the tank where the bolt once was, clean water was gushing in a constant outward flow from the tank to the floor! Since the water level in the tank could not rise high enough to float the ball at the end of the arm, the re-fill valve was triggered, and more water was pouring into the tank as fast as it was pouring out of the bottom! I knew there was a shut-off valve behind the toilet somewhere, and on my hands and knees I found it. However, that too had rusted. First it was hard to turn, but finally, after wrapping a rag around it for a slip-proof grip, I gathered the strength and elbow grease to give it a full counter-clockwise turn and suddenly it loosened. But nothing happened. I turned it clockwise; nothing. Back and forth I twirled it, hoping for a reaction; nothing. The water continued to flow into the tank, and out of it too, at a steady rate.

Once again, I stuck the bucket under there, long enough to phone the plumber for emergency service. More than anything, I was afraid it would leak through the floor and my neighbor's ceiling below me. That, more than anything, scared me. I also had visions of my daughter being the only one left at day camp; abandoned by counselors and campers whose parents had arrived on time to pick them up. I stole the plastic tubing used to drain condensation from my air conditioning unit, and quickly tried to attach it to the refill stream flowing into the toilet. Bypassing the tank, I tried to divert the water directly into the bathtub. It worked for about a minute, but the water was flowing so hard and fast, the tubing kept popping off. Despite all my best efforts, the floor was absolutely flooded and I had enlisted every single towel I owned, attempting to mop it up. I even put a few quilts on the floor to absorb the flood.

It was much past pick-up time for my daughter at camp, and the plumber had still not arrived. I needed to leave the house, but I couldn't with the water pouring all over the floor. Then, in a flash, it came to me. I knew what I had to do! As quickly as possible, I unwrapped five pieces of my daughter's bubble gum. I hurriedly popped them into my mouth and began to chew until I had a nice fat wad of gum. At the same time, I searched for and found my 20-pound dumbbell. Taking the chewed gum from my mouth and plunging my hand into the tank, I sealed up the hole left by the rusted bolt, and sat the dumbbell on top of the bubblegum to keep it firmly in place. Because the ends of the dumbbell were rounded, it would not sit flush against the floor of the tank and kept tipping over. Thinking quickly, I grabbed the cap to a can of shaving cream, and placed it upside down on the wad of gum. Securing it in place with the weight of the dumbbell, the water level was finally able to rise and signal the fresh water to stop flowing into the tank. What a relief! For a moment I felt proud of myself and admired my innovation. Then I quickly dragged the heavy wet towels to the laundry room, leaving a wide stream in my path, and put half of them into the washer. Satisfied I had stopped the flood source, I scrambled to pick up my daughter.

    I left a quickly scribbled note on the front door telling the plumber to come in and start to work. About 30 minutes later I returned home with my daughter. The plumber was already finished. New rust-proof brass bolts replaced both of my old ones and the tank was securely fastened to the bowl once again. As I paid him, I could tell there was something he needed to say. The look on his face told me he was trying not to crack a smile, and holding back a laugh. He wanted to remain professional, but could not resist commenting on what he found when he arrived at my home. "That's the most clever quick-fix I have ever seen!" Clever? Maybe it was. But I responded by saying, "Hey, desperate times call for desperate measures!" (even if it means putting a wad of bubblegum in the toilet tank).

7 GRAM-MUM HATES YOU

Joe awakens as he looks back...
 Once when Jacqui was seven or eight years old, she told me with slight sympathy and confusion, "Gram-mum HATES you!" But as the years passed the sympathy disappeared, and she and Carly began to parrot the abusive accusations I'd heard from my ex-wife Cheryl during the marriage. My daughters called me a psycho (one of her favorites), sociopath, abusive, addicted, and said I never should have had gotten their mom pregnant! There was no justification for anything they said; it was narrative language and false allegations they adopted from their mother and Gram-mum, not based in reality of their experiences.
 I had no idea Jacqui was reporting to me she was a victim of heart-wrenching, horrible, psychological abuse while sitting around the table at their mother's home. Cheryl and their Gram-mum would mock, disparage, make fun of, and complain about me, their daddy. When Jacqui said "Gram-mum hates you!" my instinct had been to comfort and assure her that I wasn't hurt by it, and that "it's ok, Daddy doesn't hate her back. Daddy doesn't hate anyone." I regret now I couldn't see it for the abuse it was or how much it hurt and truly damaged the minds of my children

from a very young age, and began way before the divorce occurred.

Eventually my daughters' mangled emotions became toxic, glaring at me for attending their graduation ceremonies and refusing to accept my gifts to them, so they could tell everyone they received nothing from their dad for graduation. A narrative that one parent must be discarded had been created for them to fulfill to prove loyalty to their mother. Interspersed with their teenage years were good, happy times with me often including their friends in our home and on vacation with us. But those days could be followed by days when they said things like "If you die, I won't even go to your funeral!" I tried hard to let it roll off my back and to keep moving forward in love. I made a tremendous effort to not engage in every angry conflict, no matter how hurtful their words. I tried hard, but didn't always succeed.

At the time I was unaware of cross-generational coalitions with schemes to prove their loyalty and show the world mom was all-good and dad was all-bad. But the angry outbursts of my daughters were reminiscent of vitriol I'd heard from my ex-wife in a common threat heard by other alienated parents "I will make sure the kids hate one day and you will never see them again!". She had succeeded in breaking their bond to me, their and I have not heard from my daughters for many years now. Like other children caught in this mess, they have also alienated extended family members who do not align with them in hatred, thereby missing out on great paternal love and caring, and also the love of many aunts, uncles, and cousins and many, important family festivities such as weddings, holidays, etc. It's not their fault. They truly believe whatever lies they heard about me over, and over, and over.

I am sometimes haunted by the confusing image Jacqui pointed out to of the family sitting around the table when she told me "Gram-mum hates you!". I wish I had known when she told me, how serious and abusive that behavior was and others like it from her mother, Gram-mum and step-father. I had no idea how it made an innocent child feel to hear her loving father mocked and hated by her grand-mum and a whole group including her mom. I wish there existed an early-intervention or prevention plan at that time, but I know experts are now working toward a day when those things do exist. With the work of top family therapy experts and many advocates creating awareness, education, and judicial reform, the days of early intervention and prevention are coming.

It's too hard for children to defend their love for a parent when they are being taught to hate, reject, and fear through lies, false allegations, twisted truth, and disrespectful actions of their other parent. The only way their young minds can process this kind of complex stress is to eventually agree with the embittered, lying parent and adopt their hatred, ultimately believing that the good, healthy, emotionally available, truly loving parent is a common enemy and deserves punishment. If they don't align, their unspoken fear is that they too will become a hated ex-family member. They eventually begin to truly believe false allegations told in a steady campaign that their rejected parent is an addict, crazy, lazy, a liar, spent child support money on themselves, is abusive or a fake. I too have been accused of these things including "spending all the child support money". Twisted truths and half truths are effective tools of embittered parents who often play the "money card" using child-support lies to create false narratives about the other parent.

I am haunted by the early warning signs and wish that I had a better understanding, so perhaps I could have intervened to prevent the nightmare from continuing. At times I regret I brushed it off, and took the "high-road" meaning didn't try to verbally defend the lies they repeated about me or fight against my ex-wife's behaviors, not understanding the severity. But I know it would have most likely further complicated a no-win situation if I had challenged every angry outburst against me. I thought just by being a good loving parent, the problems would resolve. Instead they escalated.

8 THE BIG BLUE CAN
Originally published in The Showcase Magazine

I put my recyclable container out with my trash can one recent Wednesday night. The next morning, as I backed out of the driveway on my way to work, I noticed to my chagrin that the fierce, howling wind had blown over one of my recycling containers. Although it remained on my property, its contents had been scattered not only into my yard and the street, but also across the street into my neighbor's yard, and into my next door neighbor's yard, into the yard of the next neighbor down, and so on. I put the car in park and left it running in the driveway, while with my high-heeled boots and purse still strapped over my shoulder, I carried the empty blue can down the street, refilling it with my recyclables strewn into just about all the neighbors' yards. Embarrassed, I wondered if I was being watched from the windows as I ventured onto properties, awkwardly retrieving my litter while the wind blew my hair in all directions and almost lifted me off my feet. The plastic container filled with air and acted as a sail, and as far as I could see down the road, my empty jars, bottles and cans were strewn across lawns, some pieces wedged between the earth and the decorative landscaping. Was there no end? Even in back yards I tiptoed through gardens, retrieving mayonnaise jars, water bottles, and empty soup cans. Finally, when I could spot no more of my "empties" in the neighborhood, I turned toward home with a gnawing sense that somewhere out there, my empty two-gallon water jug was blowing across someone's lawn like a stray balloon, perhaps a block or two over, or maybe even into the next town.

Carrying the big blue can back to my house, I thought my work was complete. Not so. While I was out retrieving my empties, the other recycling container had been toppled by a mad gust of wind and now the lid from my regular trash can was flying through the air like a giant Frisbee. Lucky, I caught the lid before garbage began flying out of this trash can too. The contents of the newly toppled container hadn't yet gotten far. Most of it was still in my yard, but I had to chase several errant, rolling plastic bottles toward the street before snatching them up in my clutches. The closer I got, the faster they rolled away from me, and switched direction with the wind at the last second as I closed in! Again I felt embarrassed and wondered if I was being observed from windows.

As I picked up the last piece from the yard and placed it into the can, it struck me. No one else's gravy cans were rolling around in the street, no one else's mayonnaise jars or plastic milk jugs were flying through the yards. In fact, no one had their recyclables out, because I was off by a week. It wasn't even recycle day!

"You gotta be kidding me" and "Oh no, no, no!" are milder versions of what I evidently grunted loud enough to be overheard in my driveway. My children, who were home from school for a long weekend, told me weeks later my frustrated cries had roused them from bed. Hysterically they had watched from the windows, validating the embarrassment I had felt. I can't help but wonder how many others were entertained that morning by my adventure in neighborhood beautification and clean-up.

I reflected with great clarity that we all have our garbage, baggage and issues we choose to keep private. We don't often dump our stuff before random people. Boundaries are crucial in all relationships, yet we don't want to erect walls that are barriers to friendships. One of my favorite American poets, Robert Frost, said "Good fences make good neighbors", but he probably didn't envision flying recyclables. My fence isn't high enough to contain such lightweight items aloft in the mighty wind. So maybe I don't have a "good fence". Even so I hope I am still considered a good neighbor!

9 FREEZER BRA
Originally published in Not Your Mother's Book

"Only you Monica, this stuff only happens to you." In the past ten-plus years as a single mother of three, I'd heard that declaration more times than I could count. I don't ask for drama to come into my life, but it somehow finds me. Freaky stuff happens, like the washing machine repairman mortifying my teenage daughter by saying "Aha! This is the culprit!" pulling her rainbow colored thong out of the pump. Or, when my lingerie got stuck on a baffle in the dryer, causing a small house fire. But like my mother before me, when I fall down, I get up quickly, and when I get embarrassed, I laugh!

My 11 year old daughter had been playing the same practical joke on me for three years; she'd hide my water bras in the freezer, then sneak them frozen into my drawer just before I'd get dressed. I'd bought them, not because they were filled with liquid, but because I could by three for less than $20.00, and they came in the most important bra colors: white, tan, and black! I'd realized only when I got home they were liquid-filled! I didn't think I needed extra padding, extra support or extra anything! (Okay maybe after giving birth to and nursing three children,

I did need underwire beneath the gel sacks.) But mostly I just couldn't resist a bargain, and that's how I ended up with freezer bras and frozen breasts!

One summer day I was particularly parched and I reached into the freezer for ice cubes, but found nothing in the ice bin. Upon closer inspection, I saw a batch of ice about to be expelled from the ice maker that appeared to have stopped mid-motion, half way through the act. Many of the cubes had morphed into a sold ice mass frozen into the ice maker. It dawned on me then I had not heard the daily grind of ice making for several days, since before my daughters left for a weekend with their dad. I gave it a tug, a tap, a slap and a few curse words but nothing budged. I turned it off and back on again. The motor started to churn, the auger jiggled for a second, but then immediately stopped. Something was preventing it completing the last segment of a full rotation to dump the ice and produce the next batch. Investigating further, I blindly reached up into the ice making mechanism and felt along the sharp metal edges of the cube separators, I prayed it wouldn't spontaneously start turning! Not one to shrink in fear, I stuck my head in the freezer for a better look.

Pressing my cheek against the ceiling of the freezer and peering sideways into the ice maker, I saw a larger frozen mass caught in the auger which turns the apparatus to spit out the ice cubes. As usual I wanted to fix this myself without calling for professional help. I didn't want to defrost the entire freezer, so using my blow dryer as a torch and taking aim, I melted as much ice as I could from around the auger. I was making progress but the melting ice mass was dripping over the frozen vegetables and strip steaks in a steady stream. "No problem, don't sweat the small stuff" I told myself. I'll clean the water up later.

I guess it was the melting process or reduced level of cubage, but something activated an automatic sensor to produce more ice. Suddenly the water supply kicked on and water began gushing into (and out of) the freezer at a rate of what seemed to be gallons per minute! It was pouring over the freezer's bottom, cascading down the front of the fridge, and streaming onto the kitchen floor! We lived on the top floor of a condominium at the time, and my biggest fear at that instant was leaking into the space of the neighbor below! Not out of empathy. I feared she'd file a claim with the homeowners association who would then nose their way into my business. The last thing I wanted was a self-important old fart interrogating me, so I knew to act quickly and not leave the water on the floor a moment longer! I ran to the laundry room, turning off the water supply while grabbing towels from the dryer to sop up the kitchen floor. Returning to my post, I threw the towels down and took another look inside the machine.

A ton of ice had melted, and now I could see my favorite water bra; Jennifer had been at it again! I could wriggle it a little but I couldn't set it free; it seemed to be frozen into and tangled with, the auger. I had to think of a solution if I had any hopes of extricating it without embarrassment of calling my repairman again. A thong in the washing machine pump, lingerie fire in the dryer, and now a bra in the freezer? He'd swear I was having wild, drunken, crazy parties or something. No, I couldn't tell him about this and maintain my good reputation. So with renewed fervor, I got back to work.

When all the ice had melted I retired the blow dryer, but still could not extricate the bra. I grabbed with both hands, put one foot against the fridge and yanked hard! Nothing. I began to think I'd have to call for the jaws of life! My only choice was to cut the bra into pieces. I had no idea what the gel-like substance in the bra's under-cup contained, and if I cut into it and it spilled out into the freezer I feared contaminating my ice supply. Would my family be poisoned? Is it worth that risk? These are the freaky thoughts you have when there's a water bra stuck in your freezer!

With pliers, snips, wire-cutters, and lots of elbow grease, I attacked the remains of my white bra. Determined, I carefully snipped away until all that remained was the underwire and a few shreds of fabric. I still could not yank it completely free. Then, after what seemed like hours of hard labor, a wonderful thing happened. I could almost see the heavens open and the white lights beam into my kitchen with the hallelujah chorus playing melodiously. The auger turned! There were no ice cubes to dump, no ice had been produced in days. The auger simply turned, and when it did, the remains of my bra were expelled from its clutches and dropped into the ice bin with a thud and a clank! It really was as simple and wonderful and beautiful as that.

I was down one bra, but I could look forward to ice cold beverages for the remainder of the summer. The two under wires attached by a shred of fabric have been preserved in our family history. They have taken their honored place in our scrap book/photo album, along with other family photos and memories of that summer, when ice was scarce. for a few days.

10 BROKEN HEARTS AND POEMS OF SOLACE

Through the Wall

I heard you crying through the bedroom wall
And it hurt enough to make my own tears fall.
Did you knowI loved, and still love you that much?
I tapped on your door to offer my touch…

I wanted to hold you and ask "are you okay?"
But you angrily screamed at me "Go Away!"
You didn't deserve that kind of pain,
I hoped you released it; when your tears fell like rain.

I wanted to curse the one who did whatever to you
But I didn't know when, how, where, or who.
So I prayed; "God, wrap your arms around her tight
Rock her like a baby, as she turns out the light.

And comfort her for me, as I hear her weep
Let my love be her blanket, as she falls asleep".
I was trying to reach you, but my prayer was all
I could offer when you cried through the wall.

Where You Are From

You are from full days at home with mother and brother,
learning love, walking, talking, and
being nursed, sung to, read to, and taught.

You are from messes made learning to color and paint,
picnics in the front yard on blankets, and
packing up dinner for sunset picnics on the bay.

You are from poetry recited while swinging,
"How do you like to go up in a swing?", and
mommy going under you.

You are from bedtime stories,
and classical music playing in your room at bedtime, and
holding time in the morning on the couch with mommy.

You are from days digging sandcastles on the beach
 and running from the breaking waves, and
running under the parachute sheet when I shook it out on the windy shore!

You are from playing on the school playground
for a week before starting school in a new town, and
your mother no longer at home all day and visits to dad on weekends and holidays.

You are from sports I coached so you would
make new friends,
learn competition, life lessons, and
the importance of teamwork for a lifetime.

You are from cooking with mom,
learning to sew, craft parties at our home, and
lots of friends at our dinner table who slept over
often.

You are from sledding, snowmen, hikes in the
woods,
vacations to Maine, California, and
dude ranches with shooting ranges and horses.

You are from plentiful school supplies,
food, shelter, clothes, and
everything you needed for success.

You are from a place where
your talents and unique characteristics were
encouraged, and
your independence was taught.

You are from being told you are loved,
what you feel inside is as important as the outside,
and
I am proud of you every day.

You are from CDs, ipods, cell phones, computers,
party dresses, proms, and
graduations from high school you didn't want me
to attend.

You are from grandparents, dozens of

aunts, uncles, cousins, a brother, and
so many others who wonder where my girls are
now.

You are from strong roots and wings,
but I never expected you to fly so prematurely,
and
with such disdain for the nest from which you
came.

The Empty Hole

"Looking for someone to fill the pool in my backyard" the post said.

I imagined the gaping hole in the earth
the huge hole once filled to the brim
filled not only with water, but with playfulness,
adventure and learning to swim and dive and stay alive.

It once overflowed with splashing and pool toys
and the sounds of family, friends and laughter,
but

it's an empty hole now
just an empty hole with now with nothing in it.
It needs to be filled now with dirt.

They are looking for someone to fill the hole.
I too am looking for someone to fill the hole.

The gaping hole in my heart
a huge hole once filled to the brim
filled not only with love, but with the everything about you.
It once overflowed, but

it's an empty hole now
just an empty hole with now with nothing in it.
It needs to be filled, but

it can't be filled by posting an ad, it can't be filled with dirt
it can only be filled with you.

If by Rudyard Kipling

If you can keep your head when all about you,
Are losing theirs and blaming it on you,
If you can trust yourself when all men doubt you,
But make allowance for their doubting too;

If you can wait and not be tired by waiting,
Or, being lied about, don't deal in lies,
Or, being hated, don't give way to hating,
And yet don't look too good, nor talk too wise;

If you can dream - and not make dreams your master,
If you can think - and not make thoughts your aim,
If you can meet with triumph and disaster,
And treat those two imposters just the same;

If you can bear to hear the truth you've spoken,
Twisted by knaves to make a trap for fools,
Or watch the things you gave your life to broken,
And stoop and build 'em up with worn-out tools;

If you can make one heap of all your winnings,
And risk it on one turn of pitch-and-toss,
And lose, and start again at your beginnings,
And never breathe a word about your loss;

If you can force your heart and nerve and sinew,
To serve your turn long after they are gone,
And so hold on when there is nothing in you,
Except the Will which says to them: "Hold on";

If you can talk with crowds and keep your virtue,
Or walk with kings - nor lose the common touch,
If neither foes nor loving friends can hurt you,
If all men count with you, but none too much;

If you can fill the unforgiving minute,
With sixty seconds' worth of distance run,
Yours is the Earth and everything that's in it,
And - which is more - you'll be mature and grown!

11 AVALANCHES OF LIFE
Originally published in The Showcase Magazine

By the time this is published, forsythia will be in bloom, and the snowy winter will be a distant memory. But as I write this now, snow is still on the ground outside my window and our last big storm is still a recent event. A week ago I went to an interactive rock music show featuring the band of a high school friend. A carful of friends followed me to the venue in a nearby town. I was bundled in a pea coat with deep warm pockets and a scarf wrapped around my neck. After some time I began to feel a bit stuffy with the heat on in my SUV, so I opened my sunroof for some crisp, albeit cold, night air.

Not until I came to an ever so gradual stop at a red light, did I remember I had never cleared many inches of snow from the roof of my car. It was covered with what I can only describe as a slushy, loose, flat snowball. When I opened the sunroof, I guess the slushy mess had moved back with the sliding roof window, and I remained unaware. I got my first clue when the car stopped but forward momentum and G-forces kept the snow on top moving in the direction I had been traveling, and when it slid its way to the open sunroof, it cascaded into the car like a waterfall of slush before I could reach up and press the button to close the sunroof.

It landed on my head, right shoulder, lap, console, and cup holders. Thinking fast as the light turned green and we were on our way again, I opened my driver's side window while driving, and began to throw large snowballs out the window. Gathering it from my lap before the heated seat melted it to water, I formed nice, icy, snowballs and threw them out, wondering what my friends traveling behind me would think of the shower of snowballs leaving my car window and heading directly toward them. I grabbed large handfuls from the cup holders and flung them. Smaller amounts from my head, hair and shoulder made their way out also. Onward we travelled with my fingers numb from cold, and snow clumps flying from my car as we drove.

When we arrived at our destination, my friends asked about the snow falling off of my car as they followed behind me. They had not realized it was coming from inside, not outside of my vehicle. When we walked into the venue, I reached inside my pockets to warm my cold wet hands, and sure enough deep inside my right pocket was a hefty amount of snow! Needless to say, my hands weren't warmed, and embarrassingly, I stood inside the lobby with handfuls of snow in my freezing fists! I quickly ducked back outside and formed one last snowball to throw into the bushes.

Other friends joined our table of 15 that night, and the evening proceeded with awesome music, laughter and dancing all night long. We had fun and I didn't think about the avalanche of snow in my car until the next day when I noticed a puddle in my cup holder. The morning sky was reflected, and I thought about how life is full of small and big avalanches.

I experienced several avalanches that winter which had nothing to do with the barrage of snow storms we were deluged with. Have you ever felt things are falling down all around you without warning? We don't usually see life's avalanches coming until we are buried deep. Sometimes we have to dig ourselves out with our bare hands and continue to move forward. Sometimes we can enlist the help of friends and family. Sometimes they can only watch, not understanding what we are dealing with. But in the end we must do everything we can to stay positive and surround ourselves with friends and loved ones to keep us dancing all night long!

12 DADDY DOESN'T LOVE ME

Sharon awakens and understands...
I remember defending her dad when Brooke returned from a visit with him at age six. "Daddy doesn't love me. I don't think Daddy loves me!" she sobbed uncontrollably. No child should ever feel their parent doesn't love them.
"Yes he does, he does" I assured her.
"But I feel like he loves Daina, and not me. He won't let me sit next to him at The Tea House like he always did. He said he was saving that spot for her."
"He loves you honey, I know he does," I offered, as my heart broke holding my child who struggled with deep emotional pain. "he just shows it in different ways that I do." I offered.
I held her close until the sobbing subsided. I tried so hard to bolster them emotionally to the extent I could, knowing a strong emotional psyche would help them in life. It did not occur to me that she feared he might hate her too, as he did me.
Like all children in these situations, my daughter was being conditioned to disparage and disregard me already. In time, she began getting a strong message it was none of my business what they said, did, bought, received, or heard while on visits to dad's house. Later, they told me that their lives at school were

none of my business, even though I had relationships with the teachers, administrators and school community. It was their father who had never, ever attended a school conference of any sort, even while we were married. He was the one who made it none of his business to be engaged in their school-life. Encouraging the kids to successfully push me out of their lives, would regulate or equalize his failings and his un-involvement. By that point in time they believed the thoughts were their own - and they still do, but they are smart young adult now, and that inspires my hope this won't last forever.

I remember a late night call from my very frightened seven year old daughter, terrorized from "rated R" haunting, horror movies selected by her father to watch together. Too afraid to sleep, she called me. I tried to calm her fears, "Go to Daddy and Daina's room, tell Daddy you're afraid," I suggested.

"His door is locked. I already knocked on it and told him I'm scared. He told me to go away and stop being a baby. I'm so scared and I'm not allowed to turn on the light 'cause Adam's sleeping. Daddy took away my night-light 'cause he said they are for babies!" Oh, how my heart ached for my little girl, but I still didn't understand she was being psychologically abused.

I felt powerless yet I came up with a solution to help my child sleep a hundred miles away from me. I suggested she bring her pillow, blanked and phone into her bathroom where she could leave the light on. I encouraged her to make a sleeping bag and get comfy on the floor. I wished so bad I could lay with her and hold her till the fear abated, but all I could do was promise to stay on the phone with her and quietly sing, or just breathe till she fell asleep on the bathroom floor a hundred miles away. And I did. And she did.

In the meantime I prayed every day as I did when they were babies asleep in their cribs; "Lord, please keep them safe healthy, secure, and happy"

13 HOUSE SONG
Originally published in The Showcase Magazine

Before the summer equinox that year, I had already learned, grown and transformed myself more in just a few months than I had over the course of years. I embarked on a series of physical, intellectual, and financial challenges. I sold my condominium, purchased a house, and began making improvements months before moving in. From the moment I'd first seen the little house, I had visions for it to be very different from the form I had found it. I rolled up my sleeves and jumped right in. In addition to working at a paint store, teaching art lessons Monday nights, and playing taxi driver to my teenagers, I was also fully enmeshed in construction projects, working late hours alone with power tools in an otherwise vacant house. I'd arrive back at my condominium covered in paint, tar and other goop before plopping onto my waiting bed. Many mornings I rose early and put in a few hours of hard labor before getting showered and dressed for my part-time job. I accomplished things I never knew I could while managing the responsibilities of motherhood, my job, my business, and attending a literary group.

When drawing my deck plans I researched construction codes, cantilever allowances, joist spans, and footing depths. I was required to specify every detail of the project from the hot-dipped galvanized nails used in each hole of the fasteners, to the copper flashing where ledger boards meet the house. I never produced architectural drawings before, nor used a Wonderbar or Sawzall, and I am accustomed to "just doing it" when I approach projects, without planning much detail. This house proved I can do things in a precise, step-by-step manner, and showed me how much I was capable of doing. On the first floor I took down several walls and erected new ones. On my hands and knees for hours, I removed layers and layers of flooring, finally opting to paint the tongue and groove subfloor and seal it with polyurethane. When I removed old carpeting from the back steps I discovered the treads and risers were rotted through, and the old carpeting had been holding them together. Disappointed, I told myself "I guess I'm building steps today," and off to the lumber store I went. with renewed enthusiasm. Over a few months' time, I transformed what was an impeccably maintained, charming little Cape Cod into a more contemporary, shabby-chic space, reflecting my personal style, and perfect for my family. With every change, my vision came to life detail by detail, while at the same time, the renovation process transformed me too, and in some ways redefined me. I also carried with me the hope that moving to a larger living space with more privacy for my daughters would quell their unexplained anger and our relationships would return to normal.

    I never wanted to be a divorced, single mom, buying and renovating a house without a partner. But my situation provided priceless opportunities I wouldn't have embraced if I'd remained married. If I still had a husband, I am fairly confident I would not be the one acquiring new power tools, learning how to use them, and presenting hand-drawn plans to the township construction office. Instead of relying on a husband, I became a bit of an architect and general contractor! I'm amazed at what I've learned and achieved, and I accept it as all good. But I remember years ago, a friend told me there is no good or bad in life - only opportunities for learning and growth. She was right.

I swapped out a dining room window for sliding doors leading to my new deck. Tucked behind the sheetrock when we opened the wall was an undated, untitled and unsigned poem or song that would have remained undiscovered for eternity. Instead, it has become a gift from the house itself, and it resonates with me on my journey, as it obviously had done with a mysterious stranger years ago:

> On the road that I have taken, one day, walking, I awaken,
> Amazed to see where I have come, where I'm going, where I'm from
> This is not the path I thought, this is not the place I sought
> This is not the dream I bought, just a fever of fate I've caught.
> I'll change highways in a while, at the crossroads, one more mile.
> My path is lit by my own fire, I'm going only where I desire.
> On the road that I have taken, one day walking, I awaken.
> One day, walking, I awaken, on the road that I have taken.

I later learned it was an excerpt from a Dean Koontz poem. All I knew at the time was how well it expresses the disillusionment we encounter when life doesn't go according to plan. It also expresses taking ownership of circumstances and brings hope that changes for the better are right around the corner; one more mile. My friend was right about opportunities for learning and growth, but I think she was wrong in saying there is no good or bad, because in the end, transforming my house alone was all good!

14 REVERSE ENGINEERING
Simultaneously published in Not Your Mother's Book Anthology, and The Showcase Magazine

When Spring arrived, I decided to enhance my outdoor living space with curtains I made from beautiful weather-resistant orange fabric with a geometric print. After fabricating the panels I determined the best way to install them was to mount them on a board with a staple gun, rather than hang them on drapery rods. In my collection of assorted tools I located not one, but two staples guns. One was standard, and the other was a desktop stapler that converted to a staple gun. Moments of frustration followed when I realized they were both nearly empty. I scrounged around and found some partial sleeves of staples and got to work, hoping they would last. I was almost finished when I ran out of staples in both guns. I dropped to my hands and knees and resorted to delicately attempting to insert stray singular staples that had scattered when I'd dropped the partial sleeves earlier. I would get one or two into the tray upright, but every time I got a third or fourth one in they tipped over and turned sideways! Arrgggh! It became painfully obvious this was not going to work! My partially new installed creations were hanging lopsided and flapping about.

I headed for the store we all know as Staples. It seemed the obvious choice as I walked in toting a gun in each hand. The store clerk was very helpful, but doubtful he would have what I needed.

"Really? Not even for my convertible desktop stapler? But I'm in Staples, aren't I?" I asked with a friendly smile.

He guided me to a tiny section at the end of aisle four. Who knew, specific staples, for specific guns? Why can't they be universal?

Together we sifted through all of the little boxes.

He mumbled. "No, this won't work. Wait, maybe this one." Box after box was considered, then each was returned to its little spot on the little shelf in the little area designated for staples at Staples. "I'm sorry Ma'am. I think maybe you should try Home Depot," he offered at last.

Home Depot? Really? That big, huge, gigantic store for a little box of staples? Luckily it was right around the corner, and although daylight was fading, I held on to the hope I could finish my project before nightfall.

At Home Depot, I found another helpful employee and asked if she could help me find the right staples for at least one of my guns. "This is what you need," she said handing me a box of 1/4" T19 staples. "See? Quarter inch, just like it says on the side of your staple gun." I thanked her, and on the way to the register I decided to double check the fit. I couldn't get them in the gun!

I spotted a tall, burly, young employee. "Can you show me how to load this gun?" I asked, feeling a bit incompetent. When he couldn't load it either, I breathed a sigh of relief.

He declared, "These aren't the right staples for

this this gun. See?" He pointed to the side of the staple gun. "Yeah, these are quarter inch, but it says here you need T20s or T25s."

Back to the staples aisle we went. He laughed when I told him I had originally gone to Staples for staples. As he picked up box after tiny box, it became painfully obvious I was not going to be able to get the specific staples required for either of my guns. But before giving up and going home discouraged, I had an idea.

"Why don't we reverse engineer this problem?" I finally offered. "Looks like you have plenty of T50 staples here. Do you sell a staple gun that takes T50s? Maybe I need to buy a third staple gun and a lifetime supply of staples to go with it."

He laughed again and helped me find a staple gun that needed T50 staples. He even unpackaged it to show me how to load it. I left the store feeling a bit excessive, carrying three staple guns and more T50 staples than I would probably ever need, but i wanted to be sure I wasn't going to go through this again!

As I hoped, I was able to hang the panels before nightfall and another home improvement project was complete, thanks to a helpful employee and some creative reverse engineering.

15 IT HURTS

A Man's Pain   A Woman's Pain

Crocuses and Daffodils

Crocuses, daffodils blooming at a house that's now a blur,
Memories of bunches from the yard picked just for her.

Not many memories endear her,
to the life she had there before,
But the unspoiled innocence of her children,
and the sound of her banging porch door.

The porch was the Narnian wardrobe,
the house and the yard were their world,
And she was the Queen of their Childhood Land,
as the bittersweet years unfurled.
As they toddled or ran from the yard to the house,
she'd hear the porch door banging.
They'd need her assurance for a minute or more,
and she was there with love unchanging.

And they came to her with flowers,
turtles, butterflies, frogs and bugs,
And boo-boos and hurt feelings,
for Band-Aids and her endless hugs.

Band-Aids and hugs were more than enough,
to soothe what they knew of pain.
But the horizon's storm was encroaching
and she knew it was not a Spring rain.

She battened down the hatches,
for as long as she possibly could.
She'd protect them from what was coming,

from the pain only she understood.

And she'd hold them and kiss them, and love them forever,
and send them back out to play
But she knew their unspoiled innocence,
would come to an end soon one day.

And she prayed she'd be able to see them through,
it would take more than Band-Aids and hugs,
To heal pain that might haunt them forever,
as they handed her flowers and bugs.

Crocuses and daffodils tell her,
of a time she still dared to believe
When hope sprung eternally in her breast then,
and now she is not so naïve.

They left the house with the flowers,
and she held them tight while they cried
Starting over again in a faraway place,
while she taught them her strength and pride.

And together they made the transition,
through changes brought by the years
And they leaned on her and she held them up,
and she kissed and wiped their tears.
It's been a long time since she heard or felt,
the pulse of that banging screen door
When they came to her to feel centered,
and went back outside to explore.

Like a bridge to the joy and pain of life,
how it spoke to her with its sound

It was the heartbeat of her children,
as they came in and out and around.

The yard of crocuses and daffodils;
alas she no longer calls "mine".
And the kids visited step-family,
in that house now left behind.

And the hands of time keep turning,
and Spring comes every year.
Flowers bloom in the same yard again,
even though she no longer cares.

But no matter the season, the place, or time,
beauty was and is still always there.
And her children are like the Spring flowers,
blooming without her somewhere.

Dirty Snow

She didn't kill the babies in the nest on the mountaintop, but she destroyed something inside them. She began early, little by little, bit by bit, bundling them in something like dirty snow, packing it around them, separating them from the warm paternal bond.

"He's bad, bad, bad. I'm good, good, good. He's worthless. He doesn't love you, he only loves himself. Why do you love someone so worthless? He's disgusting! You can't trust him. He steals the child support money. You can't trust anyone in his family; they don't like you. They all think they are so great. They're not great. They're bad people. They're selfish, they're liars, they're fakes. You'll see!"

Finally, cocooned in snowballs of manipulation, abuse, lies and hate, swallowed up in confusion and chaos, they needed only a small push downhill. So small, they didn't feel it. They didn't know she had packed the dirty snow and gave them a final push. Their father didn't know either.

"What's going on? What's wrong? What's happening to my sweet, loving, kind, caring, generous girls?"

From the mountain top, he wailed "Nooooooo!" wishing he could save them, wishing he could stop gravity.

"I'm sorry. I'm sorry. I'm sorry. Stay. Don't go. I

love you. I'm sorry for anything I ever did that hurt you. I love you!" But they could no longer hear him.

She'd enlisted them in her army against him and convinced them he was lying. Dizzied and dizzier they became as they abandoned the nest where they'd become honors scholars, athletes, generous, kind, hard-working young adults. Dizzier and faster they rolled and bigger grew the snowball of hate, manipulation, and lies with every foot of descent.

More powerless he became as the chasm widened. As momentum built, they no longer knew how or why they were rolling so fast and far away from him.

With a smug smirk, she watched and waited in the pit at the bottom. She caught the huge snowballs in her arms, and in the chains of irrational, twisted love. "I am good, good, good. He's worthless!" She repeated the oft heard refrain. They were fearful and afraid of the love at the top so far away now. But she felt secure they could never roll uphill to the father who was surely a broken mess.

They had changed. Something inside them was obliterated. They had no path, no way, no desire to begin the long, winding, scary, ascent to even visit the nest from which they came, and for which they had only disdain.

He prayed for the dirty snow to melt and she,

finally feeling secure in their love for her, prayed it never would.

No More Us, No More We

Right now, there's no "remember when",
no more "us", and no more "we".
I pray you don't forget what used to be.

I would never believe it could shatter and break,
the normal healthy bond we had before.
But now, there's no "us" or "we" anymore.

I wasn't perfect, but I didn't break it,
you were manipulated, abused and lied to.
I can't fix it, though I tried, tried, and tried to.

Now I'm waiting, waiting, waiting, till you know,
it's never too late to make a new start,
and find your way back home in your heart.

Backache/Heartache

16 THINKING DREAMS

Wednesday, April 30, 2014

When I was awakened by a phone call this morning, I had been dreaming of Amy and me. Poor baby. I love her so much. We were in an unfamiliar place and I had just purchased tickets to an event, when I saw her. She had come to make a purchase as well. Between us was an amicable tension we both tried to politely dance around. I wanted to acknowledge her with love and guide her to the ticket line. I was asking if she wanted me to stay with her in line or leave, keeping more physical distance between us when the phone rang and I woke from the dream. That seems to be a theme in my dreams about her and Jennifer. I want to be there for them, but only if they need me. I want them to be strong and independent when they are ready. Those are my dreams; this is also my reality. I did not cling tightly to them. I tried to give them strong roots, but let them fly with wings just as strong.

Since Sunday evening, I've had dreams about both Amy and Jennifer. In the dream with Amy, she needs me to give her guidance. She wants to know where the ticket line is. Evidently she is buying tickets to the same concert for which I just bought tickets. We have the same taste in music. I walk her to the line she is seeking, very aware I do so on eggshells. "I'll just be over there," I tell her as I begin a tentative retreat. She looks up. "Unless you want me to stay on line with you? Whatever you want," I offer. I can see she is struggling internally; struggling with wanting and needing me, but not knowing if it's safe. We are both trying to have a relationship. We both want it; we both try hard.

In my dream with Jennifer, we are in a foreign land. I don't know if it's France or Italy. Jennifer knows her way around well enough to guide me. I know I sent her to Italy for two weeks in High School; perhaps that explains her familiarity? Then I recall I have no idea where Jennifer has travelled in the past several years. How would I know? It is possible she's familiar with Paris and other European cities. When I acknowledge this, I realize I still have no idea where I am. But I am in her world. And that's what matters, and that's a good thing.

Field of Dreams, Monica Giglio

17 CHRISTMAS ANGEL
Originally published in The Showcase Magazine

I'd forgotten all about the to-go plate of food I'd spontaneously prepared for the delivery guy who came to delivers flowers to my home last Thanksgiving. It had been cold and rainy as I attempted to answer the doorbell with greasy hands and saw his car was in disrepair. He wore a hoodie, baggy jeans, dreadlocks and appeared to be from a different kind of town and neighborhood. When I could not take the glass vase of flowers in my slippery hands, I invited him and wondered what it was like for him delivering all day to homes a-waft with the delicious smells of holiday dinner cooking, while he worked delivering flowers. He waited while I washed my hands in the kitchen sink so I could get his tip from my purse.I think I even asked "Do you get to have Thanksgiving Dinner with your family today?", not knowing if he had parents waiting for him, a wife, siblings or friends to share the holiday with. Just before he turned to leave,I quickly prepared a to-go plate of food for him. I had cooked two turkeys, and the first one, a teriyaki turkey, was already carved as I waited for my guests. On a paper plate I put a few slices of white and dark meat, some cheese puffs and sausage bite appetizers. And then I forgot all about it until Christmas Eve.

As the church candlelight service ends, a tinge of loneliness mingled with sadness overcomes me. I miss my son in California with his wife, and especially my daughters celebrating without me another year. An old friend knows how I must feel because when he wishes me Merry Christmas, he hugs me and doesn't let go all the way. Tears fall, and I don't even try to suppress them while he keeps one arm around my back and offers kind words as I lean into his shoulder. Finally, I head to my empty home in a quiet reflective mood. For the first time in my life I didn't put up a Christmas Tree because there would be no gifts under it this year; not even one. But I had my little cry at church, and I was determined to have a joyous holiday - no more crying.

I turn onto my street and see the twinkling lights I'd put outside. I stop at the mailbox at the end of my driveway. Reaching into the darkness I feel a few Christmas cards; I can tell by their size, shape, and weight. Inside the kitchen, I open a sweet card from my mom with a gift and I am thankful for her and family love on this Christmas Eve night. I do not recognize the handwriting on a thick envelope as I open it to find not one, but two cards. One is signed by "your delivery personnel" and then his name. For an instant, I wonder who is this from? My mailman? Taking up the entire left side of the other card is a neatly printed note that begins:

"Dear Monica Giglio, On Thanksgiving you invited me in and gave a generous tip for the flowers I delivered, and gave me a plate of delicious food. I asked about your busted up internet router and you smiled and said 'it still works'. I replied 'That's all that matters - it still works'. Now, this is just me, thanking you for that moment - for sharing part of your Thanksgiving with me..." His note continues to express gratitude and calls me a saint many times over; a title I do not deserve. Now I am crying again despite my intention to cry no more. He closes by saying

"...These two songs are my gift to you, Tidings of Comfort and Joy, and We Need a Little Christmas..."

No CD or recording or even lyrics, just the mention of the two titles. Could he possibly know that his simple, but thoughtful expression of gratefulness actually brings me immense comfort and a tiding of such great joy that I spill over with tears? Perhaps I was a "saint" to him, but in my lonely moment he had just become my Christmas Angel. I thank God that my random act of kindness on Thanksgiving had brought about this late night blessing at a moment when I needed it most. I stop crying and the joy that had overcome me remains.

How could I have known when I invited him into my home, he would be transformed into an angel by the next holiday to bring me a little Christmas comfort, and joy on a lonely Christmas Eve night. I am reminded that as we show kindness to others we are spreading the love of God our creator. The same love that came to us in the form of a baby in a manger all those years ago; the love that we celebrate at Christmas. And love, the love of God, is what Christmas is all about.

18 ONLINE SUPPORT GROUPS

As with the rest of this book, names and places have been changed to protect and respect privacy of individuals, as they become educated on their awakening journey.

Kalie: Amputated Parent

With Parental Alienation we grieve and mourn our "lost" children for a long period of time. It's not the same as a physical death and a mourning/grieving period where you have friends and family who understand your pain and loss, attending services or sitting Shiva with you. It's sometimes a solitary and seemingly never-ending grief, loss, and mourning, which is why support groups (online and real-life) are so important. And then, if you empathize with your misled, lost children, you realize they are in a prison too, bound by chains of lies. They are victims and they're hurt; they have an amputated parent.

I know I feel a tremendous amount of pain for them as well as my own pain. While all of this makes Parental Alienation wounds so hard to overcome, it also makes it that much more important to overcome, and not be paralyzed or swallowed up by it. Our lives must move forward in a positive direction even though we have amputated hearts. I feel as though part of my heart is out there in the world, untethered to me, vulnerable and bleeding, being stomped on by everyone who hurts my daughters. For me, creative hobbies have always been my therapy and have given tremendous healing powers. I encourage every hurting parent to find solace, comfort and emotional healing in the arts. You might feel you don't have a creative bone in your body, but you do. Sometimes I buy a soap-making kit at a local craft store and learn to make something that smells nice and looks pretty. If you then give your creations as gifts, you make another person happy too.

Nothing can replace the joy of having your children in your life, and nothing will undo the trauma, creative hobbies have potentially unlimited healing power to help you through hard times.

Jeff: Searching For the Root

Seeking opinions on the root of Parental Alienation: We know healthy people don't inflict this kind of hatred on children. It can only be inflicted by people with psychological issues. When we chose to have children with them, we didn't know it about our ex-partners. But in hindsight, are they people who always had displayed a combination of behaviors common in personality disorders such as for controlling, restricting, suppressing, denigrating, and harming people they supposedly love? Did they assign the closest people in their lives to subservient roles? Are they "control freaks" who obsessively try to dictate how everyone in their world is supposed to think and feel? Are they Personality Disordered in the same category as antisocial, narcissistic and borderline personality disorders who believe they're better than others, failing to recognize other people's emotions and feelings? While they take advantage of others, are they also jealous of others and believe others to be jealous of them? What do you think?

Maria: Our Biggest Mistake: Having Kids With a Sick Person

I am an emotionally healthy, non-hostile, well-liked, low conflict adult. I never thought of my divorce as hostile or high conflict, because I was neither of those things. My ex-husband didn't want the role of custodial parent. He'd always refused to "babysit," his word for caring for his own children if I needed to leave them in his care during the marriage, for appointments outside the home. Hence, I had primary custody of my children after the divorce and he had them on weekends, holidays, summer vacations, etc. I raised them in a healthy environment where they excelled in school, participated in sports and church activities, and worked part-time jobs. They had tons of friends over all the time, grew to be generous and caring, and then went on to universities. Yet the most severe Parental Alienation that my lawyer has ever seen, after more than 25 years in family law practice, occurred in our situation. Yes, we went back to court a few times over child support issues, and my ex-husband hated the very few dollars he was obligated to contribute toward the kids' upbringing. He convinced my children I was "stealing" child support money, when he should not have been discussing adult, parental, or court maters with them at all. Of course his campaign of denigration also included teaching our daughters I am an untrustworthy fake, phony, and fraud; and other lies I can only imagine. This further supports what Dr. Warshack, and other family therapy experts say about Parental Alienation not being a custody issue. It's not always about high-conflict between two adults, because often one of the adults is compliant, cooperative, and generally easy to get along with, compromising and even submissive. It's about one unhealthy person who hates their ex-partner and is hell-bent on teaching children to also hate that parent who loves them. Like the rest of us here, I did not know he was so unhealthy and hate filled when I had kids with him.

Sharie: Agreeing with Root Problem
We have to recognize the root of the problem is we had children with someone capable of teaching their child to hate, distrust, disregard, and disparage another parent. Healthy people don't do that to their children, only sick people do that. And they can do it on weekends and holidays if they don't have custody. I am not sure how a therapist can achieve deprogramming, unless the child is separated from the sick person for a period of time with NO contact with the child. Otherwise the sick parent will sabotage the whole thing. They will tell the child the therapist is a fake and a quack, shouldn't be trusted, etc. They will turn the tables and tell the child the THERAPIST is the brainwasher and in cahoots with the good parent. Remember we are dealing with sick people who stop at nothing to be the "winner" of the child's mind and brain.

Jeff: Did It Happen to You Before It Happened to Your Kids?
While in a relationship with people who have a deep self-loathing, many spouses experienced assaults on their self-esteem; a campaign of denigration

targeted at them, even before their children were born. Did they damage or destroy your self-esteem, to the point you also hated your life and yourself? Because they hate themselves, they don't want you to love yourself or anyone else - they want you to hate yourself too in their effort to convince you that no one else will ever love you. Did they make it difficult, painful or impossible for you to have supportive activities or relationships with family and people who loved you? If they were able to make you, an adult hate yourself or make you avoid the things and people that made you feel good about yourself, and the people who loved and supported you, it's because destroying those parts of you is their irrational way to lift their own self-esteem, and make you loyal to only them.

It make me sick to recall loyalty tests my ex-wife executed. At the time I felt too emasculated to continue arguing against her bizarre requests, and I acquiesced to leave our infant daughter home alone while we went for a walk in the neighborhood. I was mocked for my paternal extinct to never leave any chid alone in a house or anywhere. She convinced me it was completely safe, the house is locked, we'd be back soon, and I was a sissy for worrying. I was too exhausted to keep arguing knowing I would endure the silent treatment or other form of psychological abuse if I'd refused to leave the baby home and go for a walk. Looking back now, I should have said "Hell no. I am not leaving our baby alone!" The same thing happened when my parents traveled from two hours away to visit us at our home. She insisted we take the baby for a walk in the woods just prior to my parents' expected arrival. She berated me for arguing against doing so, convinced me to leave a note on the door for my parents in case they arrived sooner than expected, but promised me we'd be back before they arrived. We weren't. I think she enjoyed seeing my internal struggle, and my awkward apology to my parents. In each case I felt I was in a double-bind, and the most drama-free choice was to agree with her, and do what I knew was wrong, just to avoid her psychological drama or abuse. It's embarrassing to admit I relinquished control of my own good decision making to her, and I was an adult! My kids are just kids, so I can see how easily they can be psychologically controlled by a person like my ex-wife.

If they can make us, as adults, prove our loyalty to them by presenting bizarre choices, and not backing down, how much easier to make a defenseless child hate and reject you, and the other people in your family whom they love and are loved by? It's what our unhealthy exes NEED to do, so that when they eliminate everyone else, and loyalty tests are passed, they themselves can feel loved. It's not rational. The unhealthy psyche is the root of Parental Alienation (and many other abuses). In the unhealthy, and often subconscious logic, if they can get the child or children to hate you, it guarantees they will be loved, thereby quelling or regulating their deep feelings of human inadequacy and fears of abandonment.

Kevin: Administrator of his own online support group

Dr. Steven Miller, MD and Parental Alienation expert has it right; there is a huge difference between moderate and severe alienators. He says 99% of severe Parent Alienation is caused by cluster B disordered people. But since most cluster B (borderline, paranoid, narcissistic, sociopath) parents will never set foot in a therapy office, (and if court-ordered to go, they will mimic normal behavior) how does that disordered person even get diagnosed, or more importantly, the help they need? In most cases they never will be diagnosed, but the evidence of their behaviors or disorders are displayed in the children, usually caused by the psychological abuse of parents with some or all cluster B personality disorders.

These disordered parents have and/or will cause two-way pathological enmeshment in their children. Their hatred of the other parent is enmeshed into the child's mind so severely, the children believe they came to this conclusion on their own, when there is absolutely no justification for their hatred and their unusual desire to completely disconnect from a normal, loving parent. Top family therapy experts refer to this as the "Independent Thinker Phenomenon." The child is stripped of the critical reasoning skills to make their own assessment of the loving parent with whom they once shared a loving, healthy bond. If pressed for reasons why they hate the other parent, they may offer frivolous explanations such as they don't know how to cook, they chew their gum too loudly, they are "crazy", they don't pay enough child support, or they steal all the child support money.

In these severe cases, access to each parent does not give a child a chance to make their own assessment of both parents, and that's because there is a constant drip campaign of hate coming from one parent who has triangulated the child into their coalition. It can contribute to severe cognitive dissonance and no child can overcome that kind of confusion. Cognitive dissonance is the psychological confusion caused when the lies told by one parent contradict the experience the child has with the other good, loving parent. For example they are told their parent is stingy, but they experience the parent being very generous It is NOT overcome by access. In severe alienation caused by disordered people, 50/50 custody and access alone will not prevent or solve the problem. If you understand the complexity of severe cases, you understand access does not solve the problem; in some cases it makes it worse because the coping mechanisms the children must employ, add to the toxicity. They must agree with the lies and adopt them as their own thoughts to quell and process the constant confusion. There are many experts who say unless the children have a 90-day period of no contact with the alienator, just as in cases of other abuse, and intense 4-day therapy, there is almost no hope of recovering.

Severe alienation is not about custody. Access blocking might be a symptom of alienation, but modifying and enforcing 50/50 shared custody will not prevent severe Parent Alienation. When children are taught, even with limited access, to not give or receive love from a normal parent and that entire side of the family, those sweet little children have to deal with overwhelming cognitive dissonance and constant psychological confusion. They have no understanding of how to resolve it except for aligning with the disordered parent. The child's enmeshment with the feelings of the disordered parent is not based on their experience with the other parent. In fact, the child's experience with the alienated parent is almost all good, natural and healthy. Yet because these children are shamed, mocked and psychologically punished for showing love, affection and yearning for the other parent, and rewarded for showing disdain, disrespect and disregard, they begin to experience fear about their good feelings toward the normal parent. They are taught to, and rewarded when they hate, disparage, and belittle the normal parent. They are empowered and emboldened to be disrespectful, disobedient, and diminishing. Eventually they become intolerably uncomfortable in the presence of the normal, healthy parent, and this actually gets worse with time. They are too young and immature to make their own assessments, as some advocates of 50/50 custody believe. Disordered parents with access to children on weekends and holidays will shame, mock and emotionally punish their children for loving or wanting the other parent, while rewarding and affirming them for disrespect, disobedience and disparagement of the healthy parent with whom they have a right to love and be loved by.

Try to imagine it. Try to imagine being ashamed of your good feelings toward a loving parent; how would you as a young child, deal with it? How would you respond if you were mocked and made fun of by the disordered parent (and step-family, if there is one) for wanting to speak on the phone with the other loved parent? You would be lied to by your disordered parent who has the power to convince little children that a good parent you enjoy a loving relationship with, is to be feared and never trusted. You would be taught to despise that parent without justification. Even though your actual experience with that targeted parent is mostly good, natural, healthy and loving, the disordered parent is capable of brainwashing you to believe that it's all an act. You would be taught the normal parent is psychotic, sociopathic, drug addicted, etc., and the alienating parent can accomplish this with ZERO documentation or evidence-based proof. Can you imagine how you as a child would overcome that?

The children are taught the good parent is a fake who will turn on them as soon as they are trusted, and the disordered one is the only parent they can trust. They are eventually convinced only the disordered parent can shed light on the secret "truth" about the normal parent. This puts the child in a horrible double bind. If they trust their own feelings and their actual experience with the good parent, they are betraying the Cluster B parent, thus having to acknowledge their parent has lied and is still lying. That is almost impossible for a young child to do. They grow up not being able to trust their own feelings or able to make reasonable assessments of parents and others who genuinely love them. There is almost no way out for the children, because the disordered parent has already brainwashed them into believing they are the only one who can help them see the "truth".

While we may not have the skills and expertise to diagnose a person who never commits to therapeutic help, we can see our children have been severely mind-controlled. Most adults wouldn't know how to resolve or process such overwhelming feelings of cognitive dissonance thrust upon these children. There is so much contradiction in what they are taught by the alienating parent versus what they are experiencing. The coping mechanism most children affected by Parental Alienation adopt, is to align with the alienator. This forces them to become enmeshed in the hatred toward the other once-beloved parent. Children develop this hatred even while living with the good healthy parent if the cluster B parent is able to gain access, power, and control over their minds. There is a HUGE difference between custody battles and severe alienation.

Jean: I have a 21-year old and for me, not only has the alienating process robbed my daughter and me of a normal loving relationship, it has destroyed most other important relationships in my life; friends and loved ones I once relied on for support and balance. I am finding it very depressing and difficult to function in any normal way and it seems like our judicial system just doesn't care. I don't know if there is a Heaven and a Hell. I guess we won't really know until we are dead, but I would give anything to escape this living torture we alienated parents are forced to live. I don't believe this was God's plan our children or any of us. My pain is overwhelming, but knowing that my daughter has been subject to psychological abuse, makes me sick and takes the very breath right out of me. These people are her father, grandmother, aunt and uncle. They are trying to destroy me and my beautiful angel; for what?

Me: Jean, You are correct, it's not God's plan but He gives us free will and some people use that free will in the wrong way to influence the minds of their young children repeatedly. Yes, I too, empathize with the pain, fear, and confusion in the minds of these sweet children who once had a normal, loving relationship with me, with you, with all parents who've been alienated from their children. The poor kids are so hurt, so afraid to love again the parent to whom they were once so close. I feel their pain too and sometimes that pain is harder than my own. But the other parent who did these things needed to, because of their own disordered mind. For that parent to feel their child loves them, they need to induce and teach hatred for the normal parent. They are driven to make the children hate, so they can be sure they will be loved. It's very messed up. I pity all of them. They have misused their parenting influence and destroyed a part, a very good part, of their children and made them ashamed of loving that other parent and their side of the family. But we must rise above. We must find purpose and happiness. We owe it to ourselves to grow, and be strong and find happiness. It's not easy but we owe that to our children too. Chin up!

Kris: How do you keep going, day after day?

Me: Kris, I do it by working hard to make my life happy and by moving forward in a positive direction. Art and faith have a lot to do with it, and I am thankful for what I had with them before they left; before they were persuaded I should remain the target of their hatred. I think of a song recorded by Garth Brooks.

The Dance
    Looking back on the memory of
    The dance we shared 'neath the stars above
    For a moment all the world was right
    How could I have known that you'd ever say goodbye

    And now I'm glad I didn't know
    The way it all would end the way it all would go
    Our lives are better left to chance I could have

missed the pain
But I'd have had to miss the dance

Holding you I held everything
For a moment wasn't I a king
But if I'd only known how the king would fall
Hey who's to say you know I might have changed it all

And now I'm glad I didn't know
The way it all would end the way it all would go
Our lives are better left to chance I could have missed the pain
But I'd have had to miss the dance

Yes my life is better left to chance
I could have missed the pain but I'd have had to miss the dance.

Me: Yes, Kris, I know how badly this gaping, open wound hurts yet I am grateful I mothered my daughters. I had the opportunity to build emotional strength in them, as well as emotional maturity. I know there is no way I could really prepare them (or myself) emotionally for being made to feel afraid and ashamed of loving me. But I do think I helped them be strong through it, even though they chose to go along with the twisted lies. They HAD TO choose that, just as do all these poor children. It's a coping mechanism to calm all the confusion and cognitive dissonance. It's not their fault. Kierkegaard, the theologian and philosopher said our "life can only be understood looking backward, but it must be lived FORWARD". So like the song says, I am glad I didn't know. And I'm glad they haven't fallen apart and are so far strong young women with deep roots and independent wings. I'm only sorry they flew so prematurely with such disdain out of the nest from whence they came. But yes Kris, I am glad I had the chance, and the dance...

Marty: Untitled

All of our stories are so similar, with only minor differences. In Mike Jefferies's book, *A Family's Heartbreak*, he does a great job explaining how the alienating parent usually has psychological issues that pre-date the divorce. It makes perfect sense; only a sick person would want to destroy a loving parent-child bond. I know now the only way Parental Alienation could have been prevented in my family would have been for my ex-wife to have no contact whatsoever with our son and daughter, until she'd gotten the help they needed to understand children need to be free to love and be loved by both parents without shame or condemnation. Instead, I was encouraging and helping them have relationships with their mom and and the entire stepfamily whom I shopped for with my children at holiday time.

My ex-wife and I shared 50/50 custody but she was still able to brainwash my poor children to believe I am a person to be avoided at all costs. All the while I was loving them, creating a great home life in a great suburb, coaching their sports, providing great health care, encouraging friendships, aiding their religious/spiritual development, she was simultaneously chipping away and eroding my relationship with my children. They became more and more toxic and empowered and encouraged to disrespect me as their teenage years progressed. They eventually cut off all forms of communication with me, even though they could not articulate their reasons for their intense "all-or-nothing" hatred.

I remember receiving a call from my 10 year-old at his mother's house years ago. Sobbing uncontrollably he told me that my ex-wife and her new husband held him down by his arms and feet and encouraged his sister to take a swing at him. He could barley get the words out, crying for me to come get him. My ex wife felt justified in this form of "discipline". My son was rough-housing with his sister and my ex-wife got annoyed and felt she must "teach him a lesson". Again I felt powerless to stop the abuse of BOTH children and the horrible situation she'd them in. I wanted to go rescue them both. But it was the middle of a historic snow storm, roads were impassable, and set of emergency had been issued by the governor. Powerlessness overwhelmed me. The following week at school, my son shared what happened at his mother's, and a mandatory investigation by State Child Protective Services ensued. This enraged my ex-wife who postured self righteousness and defended her choice of discipline, but deep down feared her parental inadequacies would be exposed. She punished my son for violating her code of silence about activities occurring at her house and refused to see him for the next 3 months. Eventually she altered the story to accuse me of making my son report the abuse.

I mention all of the above as a caution to all of us - the courts can't heal the psychological issues of the alienating parent. Custody issues may be solved in a courtroom, but a severe alienating parent can be so good at what they do, that they can manage it even if you have equal access and custody of your children.

Mike Jefferies says in his book that, "Coping with

and accepting the enduring loss of our relationships is made easier when you understand intellectually what has happened." Staying open, loving and strong, and maintaining a joyous life, is a daily challenge. But we can do it! Hang in there everyone and don't let Parental Alienation take you down into depression. Get the help you need to smile every day!

Kara: My Mother Committed A Felony

I stopped the car at the end of the driveway, rolled down the window and reached into the mailbox. I placed the mail under my arm as I parked, grabbed my things and entered through the kitchen door, then placed it on the counter while I began making dinner. Later I went through the pile; mostly junk mail and some bills I recognized by the unique envelopes in which they were sealed. Because I knew it held my cellular phone bill for my children's and my phones, I opened the red and white envelope. When I saw the charges, I wasn't sure what, but I knew something was wrong. There was no credit shown for my last payment, the charges were unusual, and there was only one phone line listed. There should have been four lines, one line for each of my three children and my own. I was confused, frustrated, and just a few seconds from calling to ask what was going on, when I realized I didn't recognize the phone number they were billing me for. It was sent to my address, but this bill was not mine!

Before calling the phone company about their billing mistakes, I called the phone number they were billing me for and I heard my son's voice on a voicemail recording. Oh my gosh! I looked back to the bill in my hands and saw, although it was addressed to my mailbox, it was indeed in his name.

In that moment, I realized my teenaged child, an honors senior in high school, basketball player with a part-time job, had evidently, secretly gotten a new cell phone account of his own. A sense of doom overcame me. I knew he would not take it well when he found I called him but there was no way of undoing it now. Obviously he hadn't wanted me to know he set up his own account and purchased a new number; I'd been providing his cell service for years. I knew he'd be angry about being "outed". But it was an honest mistake, and I thought it was best to let him know by sending him a text, although I could predict the bad repercussions.

He ignored my text, but after speaking with his father, his response was to cite laws stating it's a federal crime to open someone else's mail, thereby proving I was a criminal! He screamed and hollered that opening his mail was a federal offense and I deserved to be in jail! Then influenced by his dad, he began to tell anyone who would listen that among other things, his mother should be raped in court and is a felon who deserves punishment for this crime.

Don: Three More

We are all familiar with the list of eight Parental Alienation criteria that indicate a child is being taught to discard, hate and un-love a parent. But I wonder if two or three more line items should be considered in the lists of common strategies or common behaviors of severe alienators:

1) They usually are alienators before their children are born. I see a common thread of disordered people alienating their spouses from the people that love them - their close friends and family. Their sense of being loved seems to be so deeply

threatened by their spouse's other supportive relationships, they are driven by a strong inner force to make it painful for their spouse to have friendships and support systems outside the marriage. Eventually, the targeted spouse (us) gives up and becomes alienated from the people they love, who bring joy to their lives. Having mastered this with an adult, it's easy to also do it to their children. First they need their spouse to love only them. Next they need their children to do the same - love only them and hate the target parent and their whole family who bring joy and love to the children. A version of this pattern before the children enter the equation seems to appear in almost every story.

2) Since money is something tangible, and something kids relate to, alienating parents seem to almost always use it as an excuse. They neglect the children's needs then make the hurt caused by it the other parent's fault. Accusing the other parent of not paying child support or "wasting" all the child support money and spending it on themselves, seems to be another weapon in their arsenal of alienation. Not only does this allow the alienating parent to selfishly neglect the child's needs and wants (whether it be college, a car, toys, clothes or even food), this lie, when it's believed by the children, taps into the their feeling of powerlessness. It projects into a tangible way to make the the children believe it's the targeted parent who is the selfish one. As with most alienation strategies, t's one of the easiest ways for the disordered parent to deflect their own self-centered stinginess, and classic projection of their own inner demons onto the other parent. It's another way to get the children to align with them in victims of the hated, targeted parent. Lying to kids about a their other parent's money management seems to also appear in almost every Parental Alienation story.

3) Alienators use the "fake and phony" message too. When an aliening parent has no material to use against the target parent, they begin to tell the children the other parent's goodness, kindness, and love, are all just part of one big act, and they will turn on them at any time like Dr. Jeckyll and Mr. Hyde. They teach their children everyone else in the targeted parent's life has been fooled, because the targeted parent is nothing but a fake and cannot be believed or trusted. This planting of suspicion and secret knowledge that the targeted parent as a fake, is present in many, many stories.

Maria - Post Traumatic Stress

I think with severe Parental Alienation, we all have elements of Post Traumatic Stress or PTS. And I think 'back to school' time after summer is one of the times (among others like holidays, birthdays, etc.) that PTS is triggered. We once had a healthy relationship with our kids and lovingly helped them back to school. Like all parents, we shared their excitement for the upcoming first day each year. We shopped for Hello Kitty or Ninja Turtle backpacks and lunch boxes. We bought Lunchables, made ham and cheese roll-ups, or whatever fun, healthy food we could think to send in their lunches. We bought brightly colored folders and stickers. We thought hard about whom to list as the other caring adult on their emergency contact card if we could not be reached. But mostly we ourselves could be reached, and we picked them up from the school nurse when they were sick, brought them home and tucked them into bed to rest or took them to the doctor. We met their teachers and partnered with them in education. We were strong when our kids were weak.

Back to school excitement comes around every year. But instead of it filling us with wonderful happy memories, we are confronted with the reality of what ensued after all the parental love, attention, and devotion was shared. In severe Parental Alienation 'back to school' time confronts us with the grotesquely un-natural reality that our bond of love was severed. That's really bad. That's really traumatic. Post Traumatic Stress is triggered.

Ongoing stress hits us with another traumatic reminder in those moments like witnessing a decapitation. The bond of love was replaced with something else unfathomable. We became targets of our children's hatred. Some of us may have already known how it felt to become a target of their spouse's hatred. But even if that feeling was known to you, there is nothing in the world that can emotionally prepare you to be a target of your own child's hatred; the child with whom you once had a normal, healthy, loving bond.

No matter how strong, no matter how great your coping skills, no matter how great your ability to overcome and have joy in your life, these annual memories of happiness and love are now mixed with the trauma we are still experiencing as we march on through life with the knowledge of our children's hatred.

PTS or PTD? For me I think it's like a Post Traumatic Depression, and sometimes it blindsides me and knocks me off my feet. I'll be merrily rolling along in life, dealing with the pain as best I can, actually living a joyful fulfilled life in spite of it all and then - WHAM! I'm completely hit with it. Triggers like holidays, back-to-school, even birthday shopping for my young nieces who love their Aunt Monica; everything gets tainted by this horrible syndrome. I don't know if there is a scientific or medical connection, but I think Parental Alienation leads to Post Traumatic Stress or Post Traumatic Depression.

I usually think and write with great empathy for the child, trying to understand the child's point of view, for I know they are victims as well. Something great and important was taken from them; their God given right to love and be loved by both parents. They were subtly or overtly forced to stop loving, and stop receiving love from their biggest advocate; from the person with whom they shared a very close, very loving bond. From the person who happily put them first. My kids are in their 20's and still very lost children. So in addition to feeling my own pain, I wonder if they have these triggers as well. Do they go about life and suddenly get blindsided by holidays, or back to school depression? How about you? Does anyone else relate to all of this? Perhaps the adult children of Parental Alienation in our group can speak to this phenomenon.

December 2016

Where Do You Go?
Weaponized, radicalized children carry daggers of hatred and evil
aimed at an imperfect parent to break them, squash them.

Aligned with their other imperfect parent in a vicious campaign of denigration, lies, exaggerations and twisted truths a normal healthy parent would not engage children in.

To survive emotionally they have to make a choice: believe their lying parent is speaking truth, or render that parent a liar. It's not easy to believe your parent is lying to you about someone you love and who loves you, but these children have only two options.

The unspeakable, unfathomable, unnatural and most abnormal occurs; children are taught to hate their once-loved parent. Bonds are shattered, they are trained to un-love you. It happens.

They are slowly, insidiously transformed. They adopt the other parent's hatred and make it their own. They become emotionally vested in the lying parent's legal, emotional, financial and parental destruction of you. They want to hurt you, and see you raped in court. They want to see you writhe, twisted and breaking. They want you punished for the perceived criminal you are. They become disgusted with you. Then they want you gone. They want nothing to do with you or anyone in your family and they believe the lies are real without evidence, without justification. They want to never ever again see or speak to you, or anyone who knows and loves you. And they mean it.

You are left without them. You are blindsided, alone, bewildered, confused and nauseous.

You don't know when they marry or have children. A time comes when you realize you have no idea where they are, and you wouldn't know if they marry and have kids or even if they are dead or alive.

Where do you go from there? Where do you go?

Betty: Every single sentence in your poem, I can relate to but when I got to the end of the part when you don't know if "they marry and have kids..." I'm only two years into this nightmare and there's been pieces of hope that kind of burned away but I still have a little piece left, and I fear one day they will look at me and not know me even though I feel I don't know them either anymore. I don't want to accept that for one minute. I can never begin to accept that because my head spins, and stomach starts jumping and then my heart is so heavy, it's just too much. I can't imagine life in this world if I don't have hope. I've been without hope along the way many times. At this moment in time, I have some left. How many years has it been for you if I may ask please?

Me: Betty it's been many years and I understand you hope your kids will turn around before they marry and have babies. And I also hope that for you. And for all the other alienated moms' and dads' children. And I hoped that for mine too. But sometimes they take the lies with them into adulthood and marry and have kids without ever intending for you to know. Yet there is still hope and it is reflected in the belief that there is purpose in suffering. Part of the purpose is helping others through the emotional maze; offering comfort and kinship. I'm actually working on a book: a collection of prose and insights to comfort PA families.

Betty: Thank you so much for your reply Monica. I am just beginning to grasp that part about purpose in suffering and have recently been overwhelmed, amazed, and even surprised at my own gratefulness in all of this suffering. Meaning I actually am reaching the point where I feel grateful for the suffering because I am understanding the wisdom and purpose in pain... I appreciate you. I look forward to buying and reading your book. Thank you.

Me: Awwww you're welcome Betty. We all have huge open wounds, life goes on; and it's up to us to make it a good life. And it's even possible to make a joyous life despite the shrapnel wounds we learn to bandage with care.

Heather: I went through this while I was growing up. But as an adult, starting at age 25, I started piecing together a relationship with my mother. Now I'm 45, and we couldn't be closer.

Me: Thank you so much for sharing that Heather. It brings a lot of hope to those of us who think our children's minds have been stolen forever. We appreciate your comments very much.

Jenny: There are no answers, are there?

Me: The only answer many moms and dads consistently conclude is we made the irreversible mistake of having our children with someone afraid their kids won't love them unless the kids hate us as much as they do. And then once the formidable force was set into motion we were powerless to stop it or to protect our children from it. I think that powerlessness is one of the hardest parts of Parental Alienation. We think we can protect our children from harm, and then find out sometimes we can't.

Tessa: Monica thank you for your hard work and for sharing your insights. I've been suffering with this for six years now. When it first started happening, there wasn't near as much support available. I am grateful for people like you who make it a little easier for the "newbies" in this situation to feel understood and to learn what is happening and why.

Me: Aww you're welcome.... I'm just learning as I go along too.... I cannot believe it's also been many years for me since my first daughter made a permanent break from me and my whole family. It's still so surreal, like a bizarre dream, and I still can't believe it's happened. But like everyone else, we find our ways to get through it and live life despite our open wounds.

Jackie: Thank you for writing this, Monica. 18 long years... my sons have grown up and became men... There has been no internet trace in a few years... You're right, a time comes when you do not know whether they are dead or alive, and you just pray and try to rebuild yourself one day at a time. Oh, how the memories flood back at this holiday time of year, for in my mind, they are still little boys.

Me: Jackie, you're welcome. May you find solace

through my poetry and prose that you are not alone in those thoughts of your alienated now-adult children.

Betty: Monica your words are gentle and speak loud and clear to me. I am starting to understand the part about moving on, or life goes on, and our choices with that and with what's left. The things you are saying about life goes on and it's possible to have a life with joy - did you always feel this way? I have yet to obtain that (it still feels out of reach). Or did you learn with the suffering and as the years went by?

Me: It was certainly hardest in the beginning when I had no clue what was going on and I was consumed with constant confusion. But I've always been one to seek purpose in suffering. And the purpose usually involves service to others. I've also been one to turn to the arts (painting and writing) to help me deal with trials and misfortunes. But it takes a very long time to let go of your identity as a parent to a person you haven't seen or heard from in years. So yes, it takes time to detach a little with love but I have refused to become stuck on it; even though there are days that it hurts like hell. And days that tears come unexpectedly without warning. But those days are fewer now and I have continued to move forward all these years despite what happened.

Rhoda: I've had this experience also. They've been convinced that "we" (targeted parents) are a threat to them, unsafe to be around. When we have had contact it seemed to trauma bond even more with the alienating parent. It's heartbreaking to be treated like a criminal just for wanting a relationship with them. I don't have any brilliant insights to share, but if it's any consolation, a lot of us know exactly what you mean.

Me: That "Trauma Bonding" term is so sickening. Your ex made it traumatic for kid to be with you and then accused you of traumatizing the kid with no evidence to suggest the kid was traumatized, except that your ex-husband was the one who prepared the kid's mind for the imagined "trauma"! Then these-exes and children bond over this imaginary trauma. wow. Ewwww! It makes me sick, almost physically ill, to read that... Actually, maybe that's not what you were saying; but it sure explains part of my past life with teenagers I suddenly didn't understand. Your comment has granted some insight. Thank you and yes. it is indeed a consolation.

Me: While the Parental Alienation nightmare (or the realization of it) blindsides many of us, it often comes to us slowly as a by-product of divorce or family dysfunction. We all have our ways of learning to cope with it. Mine has been to rely on the gifts God gave me to deal with life in a broken world; for me it's mostly art and painting, of which I have made a business. I've been able to manage the pain, keeping it below the surface with a happy, calm, loving exterior, offering myself to the world and to the future, whatever it may bring. Parental Alienation came slowly as my loving daughters spewed hatred one day and, "Mommy does this outfit look ok?" the next, before leaving home and severing ties completely. Unfortunately it leaves wounds that never heal. Open wounds and now new open wounds we have to learn to live with in order to function in a normal healthy way. God Bless us all!

Carolyn: Just Trying to Be a Mom

I have found my now adult alienated daughter Tiffany has received my few feeble attempts to contact her through the years, as "stalking" and enemy-like attacks on her life. She tries very hard to make herself invisible to me and yet through the years, I was able to send a bouquet of flowers on Valentines' day or other sentimental holiday, or her birthday, if I knew her place of employment. No guilt-inducing notes, no stalking or anything like that, just a gesture from me, which over time as she became more invisible, was sadly not even once a year.

We have to remember that although they enter adulthood, they don't automatically know they've been lied to about us their whole lives. It's not Tiffany's fault she really believes whatever lies and stories have been told to her about me. It's not her fault.

19 LIVING LIFE FORWARD

I was introduced to the following quote in a sermon at church. "Life can only be understood backward; but it must be lived forward," by Soren Kierkegaard the 19th century philosopher and theologian.

I'd heard of the term, Parent Alienation (which originally included the word "Syndrome") for years, but I think God shielded me from knowing the horrible truth it was happening to my children; forces were at work to destroy the bonds built on the joys of love, nurture, and parenting. It did not occur to me evil forces could be successful. No - not in my kid's lives! I was the quintessential milk-n-cookies mom, trying to do all the right things and loving the art of parenting. Like many others, I was a devoted mom, fulfilled in taking care of them even after divorce and doing it alone. Mostly, I had primary physical custody.

Looking back I think Kierkegaard gives a clue as to why I had to be in denial that while I was building a healthy home life and good memories with my children; someone else was systematically destroying the foundation of love I was building our lives on, and year after year, on weekends, summers, and extended holidays, he was making my girls ashamed of loving me. But I had to live life FORWARD; I had to believe the investments of love, time and sacrifice would reap strong healthy relationships with my daughters for a lifetime. I had to believe good would triumph over evil, love would triumph over hate. If I had believed the ugliest of hopeless truths back then, I doubt I could have lived FORWARD and given them the absolute best of me, right to the very end, like most other parents, with hope and belief in the return on the investments of love and doing the right things.

My ex-husband had once tried persuading me too, that I was a worthless piece of crap during our marriage, isolating me from my friends and family, and he was almost successful. Years of therapy restored how I felt about myself, but I know how a husband or a father's lies, negative words, and twisted truths can impact a wife's perception of herself, or a child's perception of their mom. I wish now that I'd never tolerated it in my marriage before and after we had children. However, it makes me understand how daughters were irrationally persuaded without any justification that I am a worthless piece of crap, they should be afraid and ashamed of any love for me, and were taught to hate me, as I almost did myself at one time.

But Kierkegaard is right. I understand it backward. I had to live it forward. It makes sense. And I am glad I lived it FORWARD; I am glad I didn't know it was happening. I feel sad they have to live with false shame for having any good thoughts or feelings toward me. I feel sad that it's gone on so long they are now afraid, but I know false fear is typical in Parental Alienation. I am sure they need me in the ways everyone needs their mom. I know they have surrogates, other adult women in their lives, and a step-mom; but they are missing out on a great relationship with a loving mother who lives forward and is so proud of them in so many ways, always has been, and always will be.

20 FIVE PHASES OF GRIEF

There are so many things I learned in nursing school I will never forget, which have come in handy over a lifetime. One of them is the five phases of grief. We studied Elisabeth Kubler Ross who'd authored the books <u>On Death and Dying</u> and <u>On Grief and Grieving</u>. Although others would come and go with lists of eight or twelve phases of grief, I like the simplicity of five phases. I completed series of helpful educational videos on each of these phases and how they relate to Parental Alienation which are being viewed all over the world.

If you've lost your relationship with your child or children, you will undoubtedly suffer a lot of different emotions. When you have no idea when you will see them again or if you will spend the next few holidays, birthdays, school days, or any days with them, it feels permanent. You will experience grief. Grieving the the loss of a living person, is known as 'ambiguous grief' for which there is no closure making it hard to resolve or understand your feelings. Knowing there are phases of grief to expect, and what they are, may help you to process the emotions of each phase as they occur. Even though there may be a day of reconciling with your child or children, grief is experienced in the present and the more you understand about, the healthier you can be. In nursing school, we used the acronym DABDA to remember the five phases; denial, anger, bargaining, depression, and acceptance, although you may not experience them in this exact order.

Denial - At first it is impossible to believe it's happening. If you are being blocked from access to your child, you may believe that when you go to court and everything will get fixed. As your once-loving child is transformed into what appears to be a hater, you may tell yourself it's just a phase. Many people (and I was one of them) deny the severity of the alienation as long as they possibly can, hoping one day will wake up and things will be back to normal. This is all part of the denial phase and it's a normal coping mechanism.

Anger - When the reality cannot longer be denied, it may hit you at first like a deer caught in the headlights of an oncoming car. Freight train may be more like it. You may experience intense anger when you realize your child has been shamed, mocked, and psychologically punished out of their relationship with you. Many people become enraged at the courts, lawyers, judges, ex-partners, ex-in-laws, and everyone who has played a role in your nightmare that you never wake up from. This is all part of the anger phase and you must keep your wits about you and seek help if you need it. Some people remain in this cases for a very long time and it can negatively impact their health. Although it's a normal phase of grieving, the idea is to process your feelings and move through this phase.

Bargaining - You may find yourself trying to bargain with yourself or God to reverse what has already happened. You may believe that if you could earn more money, or buy a bigger home, the children will love you again, or at least want to come visit. I know of several parents who tried to bargain with their abusive ex-partner by agreeing to false allegations of mental illness (or something else) on the promise that a custody dispute will be dropped. In all cases, the children were kept from them even further!Some parents feel if they give up smoking (or something else), then they'll be rewarded with having their children in their life again. They may even believe if they just ambush their child by showing up on their doorstep, then the child will realize they are making a mistake. Another kind of bargaining is tied closely with regret. Parents look back forensically and think "If only I had reacted differently to that situation, or bought more toys, or took them on more vacations, then I'd still have my children in my life." It's normal to seek solutions and wish there is something you can do to change the current reality, but you cannot remain in the bargaining phase forever. Like anger, you need to move through this stage, or you will be stuck on a hamster wheel of false bargains, false regret, and false expectations for the rest of your life.

Depression - It's hard to live a life without your child or children. Your relationship with them was the most important defining role of your life and when it's gone a piece of your identity is questioned, and many suffer from low self worth initially. It's certainly understandable to be depressed about it. Some days it may feel difficult to just put one foot in front of the other and breathe! You may have trouble enjoying the things in life that once made you happy. You may not be able to stop thinking, wondering, and worrying about your kids, and when you do, you cry. Many parents say they feel like a "complete basket case". Although depression is a normal part of grieving like anger and bargaining you must not remain there too long and eventually you will have to find things to move you beyond it. Sometimes physical exercise can help you clear your mind. Another great option is to find a support group of other parents who have been through Parental Alienation and develop friendships with people who understand because they have walked in, or are currently walking int the same shoes. If you cannot function normally, don't be shy about talking to your medical doctor for help. Most doctors have seen patients burst into tears when discussing sensitive matters and they can usually offer you some help.

Acceptance - Although you may find yourself gliding in and out of the phases grief in no particular order, acceptance is considered the final phase. It may be the most difficult phase, and it doesn't mean you never experience anger and depression again, because people experience the phases differently. When you are doing everything within your power to resolve the situation with your child or children, you may ultimately realize there is nothing you can do to change the fact the Parental Alienation has happened. The acceptance phase is not to be interpreted as giving up. Keep reaching out and hold on to hope that your child will "awaken". This phase means accepting the reality of your current loss of relationship, yet knowing things can change any day. However in the meantime, you will learn one of life's hardest lessons, and that is to accept the things you cannot change. Reinhold Niebuhr's famous prayer addresses this beautifully.

"The Serenity Prayer"
God grant me the serenity to accept the things I cannot change,
the courage to change the things I can,
and the wisdom to know the difference.

Acceptance is having the wisdom to understand the things you can change, and the things you can't. For example, you may find you cannot change the alienating ways of your ex-partner. One of the things in your life that you can change is you! Maybe it's time for a career change or more education for you. Focus on the courage to change the things you can and make yourself the best you can be and accept with serenity the things you cannot change.

The intention of understanding all five phases of grief, is that you will be able to identify the emotions you have experienced, or are experiencing now, and identifying them will help you to process and move past them according to your own timeline. Although every single phase is a normal part of grieving experience, you don't ever want to get stuck in, or stay in any negative place too long. We all know people who are stuck in anger and depression, and we can usually observe in them it's counter-productive to remain there. If that is where you find yourself, I challenge you to set a goal for of achieving acceptance as expressed in The Serenity Prayer. Acceptance will come easier now that you've been armed with the knowledge of the five phases. You can start now by saying the prayer every day, and one day I know if you really want it, you will be granted the serenity, courage and wisdom you need to move forward in a positive direction.

21 SELF-CARE

Moms and Dads, it so important when life hits you hard that you have the strength to not be broken down by the winds, the rains, the trials or the storms of life. There is really only one person who can take care of you, and that person is YOU! In this chapter you will find what has worked for me and for many others trying to keep it together and move through life in a positive direction. I've created videos on most of the subjects below which are available for viewing on my YouTube channel, Parental Alienation Survival Coach.

Physical Health
Do not neglect your physical health! If you are feeling "off" physically, see your doctor, because lack of sleep, depression and ill health all bundle together and contaminate your whole being unless you get it under control. Many parents complain they cannot sleep when they are going through the drama and trauma of court battles and dealing with difficult family situations, and "situational depression" commonly results. As we learned in a previous chapter, depression is also part of grieving. Sometimes stress brings on heart palpitations or

changes in blood pressure. Your doctor can help you with some of these things. They can also recommend therapy if you want to give that a try and believe it will be beneficial. Don't be afraid or ashamed. If you burst into tears, it's okay. They have seen it before. Life stress, and we all have it, can lead to silent illnesses, like high blood pressure, so be sure to have it checked often. Don't neglect your yearly physical physical and stay on top of your health!

Fitness and Exercise

If you can't afford a gym membership, try walks, hikes, home cardio, and yoga style stretches. For many years of my adult life, I belonged to gyms and fitness centers, and for many years I couldn't afford to. I learned how to do sit-ups and crunches with my feet tucked under a stable couch. I did cardio with a jump rope. There were years I bicycled long distances. Even during rehabilitation from surgeries I found that simple posture exercises can go a long way toward maintaining physical health. I encourage all parents to find a routine they can manage and afford. My uncle who maintained great fitness into his later years, once put it this way, "If I don't take care of my body, where will I live?"

Proper Nutrition

Say no to fast food and junk food. It's amazing how much better you feel and function when you change your diet in the direction of clean foods. Clean foods are those closest to the way they emerge from the earth with few ingredients or additives. I like to cook with color to make food visually interesting as well as great tasting. A simple, healthful, green salad is made colorful when you add red tomatoes and black olives! As an alternative to burgers, try portobello mushrooms. I load the caps with chopped mushroom stems, cheddar cheese, and mixed vegetables, then sautée in pan on the stovetop. Instead of grabbing cake or cookies, try apple slices with peanut butter. Preparing nutritional food and eating right doesn't have to take a lot of time or ingredients. These sample menu ideas contain only a few common ingredients, but lots of nutrition. These were originally published to my Facebook Group, Parental Alienation Survival Coach.

Spiritual Restoration

Reconnect with your faith roots and start attending services as you once did, or start going for the first time your life. Many parents have been turned off by hypocritical ex-partners who professed religion, but were hateful and mean. I am sorry those people tried to make you doubt your faith, but don't let them stop you from your own spiritual experiences. One of the Bible verses I repeat often, and is the theme verse for SPEAK Worldwide 501c3 is Psalm 34:18, "The Lord is near to the broken hearted and saves those who are crushed in spirit." That describes how alienated often feels. When you reach out to God, this verse promises He will be near to you, and you will find He is a great comfort. He too has been rejected by those he loves, betrayed, falsely accused, and more. He gets you. He knows how you feel. Please re-connect with your faith roots. As SPEAK Worldwide develops its local support groups with video curriculum in many cities, there is a great chance you will find them meeting in a church near you!

Hobbies and Interests

Find things to do that interest you. People who pursue hobbies and interests gain a sense of control and feeling of accomplishment in their lives. Those gains are really important for Alienated Parents who often feel a sense of powerless in their lives. Whether it's cooking, arts and crafts, golfing, working out, or anything else, you will gain a sense of purpose and completion if you commit yourself to doing the things you enjoy. Try to devote a few hours a week to something you feel truly inspired and enlivened by, and your positive energy will flow into your work and more importantly, into other aspects of your life!

Handmade Soap   Hand-built Ceramics   Hand-knitted Scarf

Natural Surroundings

Get out of manufactured surroundings and into nature; mountains, beaches or even walks around the block. A growing body of studies point to changes to the workings of our brains in ways that improve our mental health, when we visit or even just view nature from our windows. Studies are showing city dwellers have a higher risk for anxiety, depression and other mental illnesses than people living in rural surroundings. Now, other studies have found city dwellers who frequently visit natural environments have lower levels of stress hormones immediately afterward than people who have not recently been outside. For example, a Stanford University study looked closely what effect a walk might have on a person's tendency to brood. Brooding, is a mental state familiar to most of us, in which we can't seem to stop chewing over things going wrong with our lives. This broken-record fretting can lead to depression and is disproportionately common among city dwellers compared with people living outside urban areas. The study tracked blood flow and activity before and after walks through nature, in a portion of the brain's prefrontal cortex associated with cyclical fretting. They discovered volunteers who had strolled along quiet, tree-lined paths showed they were not dwelling on the negative aspects of their lives as much as they had been before the walk, backed

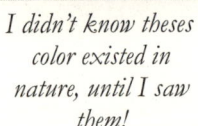

I didn't know theses color existed in nature, until I saw them!   *You'll never know what you'll stumble upon!*    *Beautiful pale teal and organic shapes lichen on a log!*

up by actual brain changes! There are many other studies to prove nature is good for your mental health and produces actual changes in the brain! While this is true for all people, those suffering the loss of relationships need to really focus on doing all we can to be the healthiest, most positive versions of ourselves we can be. So go on out there and take a walk!

22 SIX-STEP PLAN TO BE BETTER!

You have the power to choose your reaction even in the hardest trials. You must move past depression and anger and all the phases of grief. Although it may not have occurred to you before, YOU CAN CHOOSE to become better instead of bitter. These 6 simple steps will help you make that choice!

1) Accept you are powerless to change the alienating behaviors of your ex-partner. The forces that drive them to cling to hatred are deeply ingrained and unless they get help they need from a professional, they are not likely to change. Accept there are people in your life who lack the capacity to understand Parental Alienation and you cannot change their minds.

2) Believe that God is greater than you and can comfort you in your pain. Seek out spiritual leaders/mentors and make a decision to turn your life over to God.

3) Forgive: Over and over, forgive those who have permeated and damaged your child's mind, and have taught and are still teaching them to hate, reject and fear you and others who love them. Christ modeled an example of this when he prayed for those who crucified him, "Father, forgive them, for they know not what they do."

4) Self-reflect: As you learn how damaging a parent's words and behaviors toward a child can be, self-reflect on what you have said or done that may have been harmful, then ask God to reveal and remove all your shortcomings. You may not have a chance to ask your children's forgiveness, but you can forgive yourself and ask God to forgive you. He always forgives everyone who repents sincerely.

5) Pray: Through prayer and Bible study, try to improve your contact with God and pray for knowledge of His will for your life now, and in the future. As you gain understanding, pray for the power to carry out His will.

6) Help: When you feel ready, help, encourage, and comfort others going though similar situations, with the comfort and peace you yourself have received.

I developed my six step program after many years of my own struggles and working with other parents. The steps, **Accept, Believe, Forgive, Self-reflect, Pray** and **Help** are easier to follow, if you use the buddy-system. In videos, posts and execution, I've stressed the importance of meeting with others who understand because they have walked or are walking in the shoes of Parental Alienation. So your first task is to find a friend to meet with once a week, for a walk, a talk, or a cup of coffee. Although you can easily find friends in social media support groups, I urge you to meet and get to know each other in person, and of course in the safety of public places. Please grab another alienated parent and give it a try! SPEAK Worldwide is forming support groups with video curriculum in several cities, but we need more leaders, so maybe that's something you might be qualified to volunteer for?

Hang in there moms and dads. Stay strong. You are not alone; none of us are! Everyone is invited to join the closed Facebook Group, "Parental Alienation Survival Coach" with members from all over the world and follow us on YouTube Channel Parental Alienation Survival Coach.

23 TESTIMONIALS

Kansas
Monica you have been blessed with being able to say the things that Christ wants us to know.

Oklahoma
Dear Monica, …. I will continue to thank God for putting you in my life until I draw my last breath. … I'm forever grateful that you saved me from going to my grave wondering what happened to my life. I see everything from a completely different perspective. It's miraculous… I wish I could get back every dime I spent going to my psychiatrist who was worthless at gaining insight into what my issues were, so I could give it all to you. You nailed it in one day. You are the one person in my life that has made the greatest positive impact. I will thank God for your wisdom for the rest of my life…

California
Great job on the radio this evening Monica. I just wanted to send you a huge hug and thank you. Your interview actually made me cry.

My oldest daughter has been gone for 10 years. …

My youngest daughter is studying to be a nurse … She went abroad to London for the second half of this semester and is traveling to several European countries. …. I am praying for a breakthrough.

It's so hard to know they are going through so much of their life. I cannot imagine hearing that they were married or had a child. Thank you for your strength and compassion.

You are a lovely woman and I just wanted to honor you and thank you on this Mother's Day from one mother missing her children to another.

Australia

Thank you so much. You have given me a path to educate myself as a parent and also information to help me understand my frustration. God Bless!

Indiana

Thank you for SPEAKK Worldwide. I've been alienated for 17 years now, this helps to understand what's going on, I knew I wasn't crazy, I'm not alone. Thank you

Oklahoma

I already have experienced a huge burden lifted from my shoulders, and my mind. The healing has begun. I cannot express my gratitude for your strength, research, and organization. You have indeed set me on the healing path. Your knowledge and experience has sparked that paradigm shift. But now I am questioning myself... There were so many things I could have done differently, had I been educated regarding this detachment process. I studied psychology in the early 70's, in university... Had the information been available to me, I would have never allowed it to escape my awareness. And perhaps my daughter would have gained insight regarding what she experienced. But YOU have provided a healing poultice for my heart. I will forever be blessed to have been led to you. Sincerely,

California

...one great things that came from it was meeting you, you have helped me and my daughter so much...Gosh so much, the 5 stages of healing was so helpful, as my daughter and I shared areas we were stuck on, in hopes of her baby sis and two brothers coming back, bargaining, wow

We are very similar in the denial part, that's how I was with my babies till divorce, loving them with every ounce of me, and the moVing forward,

Just so many points that literally touched my heart, my daughter cried, as we mourn the people they use to be, ... You have helped me and my jo more than you'll ever know

Virginia

Thank you Monica. I respect your views very much and you bring a hopeful spirit to this 'movement'.

Michigan

...I just about 3 months ago heard about Parental Alienation and that that's what my ex and his wife have been doing to my girls. I have been praying to GOD for 5 years to show me my path and what it is I am supposed to do to help, not just me, but other families also. He showed me the end of March when I was told about "Parental Alienation Day

Norway

... so thank you again I am so happy and respect what you do for our kids going through this.

ABOUT THE AUTHOR

Internationally known artist, writer, Christian leader, and a member of the Parental Alienation Study Group at Vanderbilt University, and the founder of SPEAK Worldwide (Stop Parents Emotionally Abusing Kids) 501c3. SPEAK Worldwide is a multi-generation charity providing support groups, videos, fact sheets, and book publishing. Their 3-fold mission includes education, compassion, and spiritual renewal, and their theme verse is **"The Lord is near to the broken hearted and He saves those who are crushed in spirit."** Psalm 34:18.

Monica can be contacted in the following ways:

Facebook Group and YouTube Channel
Parental Alienation Survival Coach

Instagram and Twitter
PASurvivalCoach

Donations can be made to SPEAK Worldwide via:
website www.speakw.org

Made in the USA
Columbia, SC
12 August 2019

Your Towns and Cities in the Great War

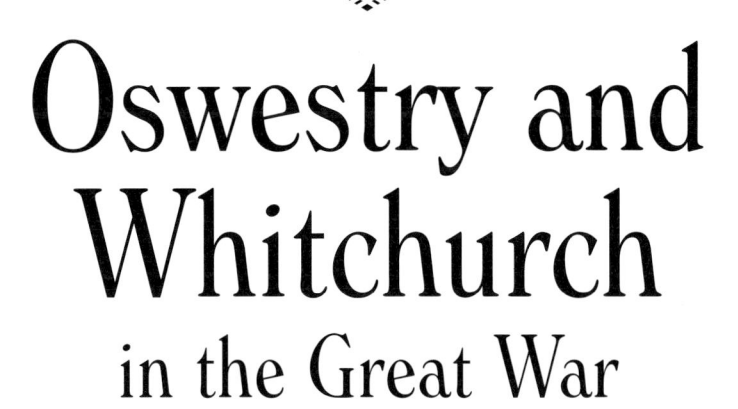

Oswestry and Whitchurch
in the Great War

Janet Johnstone

Pen & Sword
MILITARY

First published in Great Britain in 2016 by
PEN & SWORD MILITARY
an imprint of
Pen and Sword Books Ltd
47 Church Street
Barnsley
South Yorkshire S70 2AS

Copyright © Janet Johnstone, 2016

ISBN 978 1 47384 384 4

The right of Janet Johnstone to be identified as the author of this work has been asserted by her in accordance with the Copyright, Designs and Patents Act 1988.

A CIP record for this book is available from the British Library

All rights reserved. No part of this book may be reproduced or transmitted in any form or by any means, electronic or mechanical including photocopying, recording or by any information storage and retrieval system, without permission from the Publisher in writing.

Printed and bound in England
by CPI Group (UK) Ltd, Croydon, CR0 4YY

Typeset in Times New Roman by Chic Graphics

Pen & Sword Books Ltd incorporates the imprints of
Pen & Sword Archaeology, Atlas, Aviation, Battleground, Discovery, Family History, History, Maritime, Military, Naval, Politics, Railways, Select, Social History, Transport, True Crime, Claymore Press, Frontline Books, Leo Cooper, Praetorian Press, Remember When, Seaforth Publishing and Wharncliffe.

For a complete list of Pen and Sword titles please contact
Pen and Sword Books Limited
47 Church Street, Barnsley, South Yorkshire, S70 2AS, England
E-mail: enquiries@pen-and-sword.co.uk
Website: www.pen-and-sword.co.uk